A Brief History
of the Presbyterians

A Brief History
of the
Presbyterians

Third Edition

Lefferts A. Loetscher

The Westminster Press
Philadelphia

Copyright © 1978 The Westminster Press

PUBLISHED BY THE WESTMINSTER PRESS®
PHILADELPHIA, PENNSYLVANIA

PRINTED IN THE UNITED STATES OF AMERICA

9 8 7 6 5 4 3 2 1

Library of Congress Cataloging in Publication Data

Loetscher, Lefferts Augustine, 1904–
    A brief history of the Presbyterians.

    Bibliography: p.
    Includes index.
    1. Presbyterian Church—History. I. Title.
BX8931.2.L64 1978   285   78–1724
ISBN 0–664–24197–2

**In memory of my mother
Mary McClelland Loetscher**

Contents

Publisher's Preface to the Third Edition   9

1. From the Apostles to the Reformers   11
2. Two Great Reformers   21
3. The Presbyterians on the Continent of Europe   29
4. The Presbyterians in Scotland and Ireland   37
5. The Presbyterians in England, Wales, and the Former British Dominions   47
6. The Presbytery   57
7. The General Synod   63
8. The General Assembly Organized   73
9. The Plan of Union   82
10. One Church Becomes Four   92
11. The Southern Presbyterian Church   104
12. Reunion in the North   127
13. Wars, Depression, and New Life   137
14. The United Presbyterian Church of North America   148
15. Since the 1950's   157

Questions for Thought and Discussion   187

Bibliography   197

Topical Index   201

Publisher's Preface
to the
Third Edition

The Sesquicentennial of the General Assembly of the Presbyterian Church in this country occurred in 1938. In relation to that event A BRIEF HISTORY OF THE PRESBYTERIANS was prepared as an elective course for young people in the church school curriculum. The quality of the work soon commended itself to use in communicants classes, new member classes, and adult study groups. Over the next twenty years it was reprinted fifteen times.

With the union of the Presbyterian Church in the U. S. A. and the United Presbyterian Church of North America in 1958, the book was revised and enlarged, taking into account the new developments in the history during the two decades since its first appearance. The chapter on the United Presbyterian Church of North America was added at that time.

Again two decades have passed and much of significance has occurred in the Presbyterian story. Repeated plans and proposals have been made for the healing of the division between the North and the South that has now continued for well over a century. This Third Edition involves not only a complete updating of the entire work but for the first time an inclusion of material on the history of the Presbyterian Church in the United States. Whether or not the desired reunion is achieved in the immediate future, the main lines of this brief history are now complete. All members of the Presbyterian family now have an accurate and manageable resource for understanding our common history and heritage.

It is fortunate indeed that Lefferts A. Loetscher, the distinguished Professor of American Church History at Princeton Theological Seminary for so many years, who wrote the work originally and revised it twenty years ago, was able to revise and enlarge it again. With new questions for discussion, a select bibliography for further reading, and an analytical topical index, A BRIEF HISTORY OF THE PRESBYTERIANS is now given new life in this Third Edition.

1

From the Apostles
to the Reformers

A **Christian Church in a Pagan World.** The missionary success of the earliest disciples is familiar to every reader of the New Testament, the apostle Paul himself traveling up and down the Empire, winning converts in Syria, Asia Minor, Greece, and Italy. After the death of the apostles, Christianity continued to spread with amazing speed, especially among the slaves and lower classes.

In the Roman Empire the prevailing paganism was closely associated with the political government. When, therefore, the Christians refused to worship any deity except the one God, they were intermittently persecuted for almost three hundred years as traitors and "atheists." There is no nobler story in Christian annals than that of these unnamed heroes—many of them women and children —who chose death in the flames or at the jaws of wild beasts in the arena rather than renounce their divine Master. Polycarp, bishop of Smyrna, when commanded to repudiate Christ, replied with fearless dignity: "Fourscore and six years have I been serving him, and he hath done me no wrong. How then can I blaspheme my King who has saved me?" These faithful witnesses did not die in vain, for the blood of the martyrs became the seed of the church, and converts joined the courageous survivors in increasing numbers.

Christianity on the Throne of the Caesars. To Constantine the Great goes the credit for permanently changing the official status of the persecuted Christians. Legend says that Constantine, shortly before battle with a rival claimant for the throne, saw in clear daylight a shining cross in the sky with the words on it, "By this conquer." It is a known fact that, immediately following this experience, he had the shields of his soldiers inscribed with the sign of the cross, and crushed his rival in battle.

A Christian, in profession at least, was now on the throne of the Caesars. Outward benefits to the church were immediate. Christian laymen and bishops, instead of being persecuted, were advanced to positions of honor in the government. Church property was thereafter ordinarily exempted from taxation. Legislation now reflected something of the spirit of Christianity. Combats to the death between gladiators were on the way to being abolished. Marriage laws were improved. The lot of the slave was bettered. Sabbath laws were enacted. The church, with its increased prestige and wealth, was enabled to enrich its worship with the embellishments of architecture, sculpture, painting, and other arts. Christianity had become the government's pet child.

But the church's new and unaccustomed position of privilege was not an unmixed blessing. Christianity was no longer something to suffer for, but something to profit by. Following the example of their emperor, former pagans flocked to the church, bringing in with them many of their pagan immoralities and religious beliefs. The clergy became secularized and worldly. Church affairs were now entangled with court politics. Christian leaders, from their new vantage point, could use the government's authority to persecute "heretics." Some of the more spiritual churchmen looked away wistfully from the newly acquired wealth and honor to the day, now past, when to be a Christian had sometimes involved making the supreme sacrifice of life itself.

Theology. From the beginning, Christians have heeded the command, "Thou shalt love the Lord thy God . . . with all thy mind" (Luke 10:27). "Theology" is the effort to think as honestly and clearly as possible about Christian faith.

In the earliest years of the church Christian teachers were satisfied merely to repeat the language of the Old Testament and New Testament writings. But soon the deeper implications of these Scriptural statements were explored. Men asked, for example, exactly what we mean when we say that the Savior is the Son of God. Partly in order to settle, if possible, a controversy that had arisen around this particular problem, Christian bishops from all parts of the Empire met in council at Nicaea, a little town near modern Istanbul in A.D. 325. The emperor Constantine convened the meeting and himself presided. This council came to the conclusion that the Son of God was never created, but has always existed, and is of the same divine spiritual "substance" as God the Father himself. Another council, in the next century, declared that Christ has two distinct natures, human and divine, united in a single person. Thus the church endeavored, using thought forms of Greek philosophy, to assert the absolute deity of the Savior. This continues to be the official belief of all the major Christian bodies throughout the world.

These doctrines concerned the nature of the Trinity and the Person of Christ. About this time, Augustine, a keen-minded and hot-blooded man living on the southern shores of the Mediterranean, had a profound experience of deliverance, by the grace of God, from shameful immoralities and from years of groping after religious truth. His experiences and convictions, as set down in his *Confessions* and other works, were the foundation on which the church later built many of its doctrines of human sin and the absolute need of the human soul for the help of God's Spirit.

The Fall of Rome. To the north of the Roman Empire, while these theological discussions were in progress, roamed hardy Germanic tribes, disdainfully called barbarians by the highly civilized Romans. For centuries the Roman legions on the Rhine and the Danube had repelled their assaults, but in the year 410, less than a century after Constantine's conversion, Alaric, a barbaric chieftain, captured the "eternal city" of Rome itself. Before long, other barbarian hordes swept in and occupied the Latin-speaking, western part of the former Roman Empire. A new epoch in human history, the so-called Middle Ages, was beginning. The Greek-speaking, eastern part of the empire survived these attacks. Eastern Christianity, known as Eastern Orthodoxy, and western Christianity, known as Catholicism, gradually diverged more and more from each other.

The immediate damage done to the Christian church and to society in the West by these invasions was incalculable. Countless buildings, art treasures, literary works, and the accumulated wealth of centuries were swept away. Many centers of civilization were reduced to the level of semibarbarism.

Above the floods of barbarism and conquest the church stood like "a city set on a hill." In its monasteries and vaults were preserved precious copies of the Scriptures, as well as the writings of the Christian teachers, or church fathers, and classical literature of antiquity. Amid the prevailing brutality and lawlessness, the church never entirely forgot its gospel of divine love and self-sacrificing service.

Foreign Missions. In the history of Christianity there have been three great missionary, or expansive, epochs (the first two of these lie within the period covered by the present chapter): (1) the evangelization of the Roman Empire by the original apostles and the witness of ordinary Christians during the first three centuries; (2) the Christianization of the barbarians from the fifth to the eleventh centuries; and (3) the modern Roman Catholic and Protestant missionary movement, simultaneous with the commercial penetration of non-Christian lands.

The second period, that of evangelizing the barbarian conquerors of the Empire, is inferior to neither of the other periods in its importance and dramatic interest. A monk who was soon to become Pope Gregory the Great, seeing three Anglo-Saxon boys from Britain for sale in the slave market at Rome, was impressed with their handsome blue eyes and fair complexions. He asked who they were, and was told that they were Angles. He answered, "Not Angles, but angels, for they have angelic faces, and are worthy to be fellow heirs with angels in heaven." Gregory sent Augustine (not the theologian) to Britain as missionary. The half-legendary Patrick labored as missionary in Ireland, Columba in Scotland, Boniface in Germany, Ansgar in Scandinavia, Cyril and Methodius among the Slavs.

It is as a result of the labors of these and other missionaries that the great nations of Europe and the Americas today are Christian. If there be those who would disparage modern missions, let them recall the lasting effect on world history of this early period of missions.

The Pope. In the earliest years of the Christian movement relatively little attention seems to have been paid to the particular form of church government. Very soon, however, the clergy emerged as a distinct class. In order that the church organization might be strong to resist both "heresy" and persecution, bishops gradually arose, who had authority over the lower clergy.

The bishop of Rome, the original capital city of the Empire, early acquired unique prestige. When the barbarians invaded the western part of the Empire in the fifth century, and swept away the old governments, the Christian church seemed to be the only surviving bulwark. In such a crisis men desired a strong church with a strong head. The bishop of Rome was the natural man to fill the breach, and was now readily accorded the authority of pope, or "father," of the church in the West, but Eastern Christians never accepted the pope's ecclesiastical supremacy. The papacy, in supplying vigorous, even if autocratic, leadership during these dark centuries performed an inestimable service to Christianity and to civilization.

As time passed, the popes claimed increasing authority. Pope Gregory VII, in the eleventh century, claimed to be the representative of God on earth, and declared that kings and emperors held their power only during his good pleasure. Gregory was powerful enough to force the German emperor to do penance before him in the snow for three days. The papacy reached its greatest power under Pope Innocent III, in the early thirteenth century. Few kings or emperors in history before or since have wielded the power that this man held. Kings and emperors did his bidding. No man dared to contradict him. His rule marked the high point of papal power. After his time national patriotism began to awaken in Europe, and nations refused to be ruled from Rome.

Monasteries. Back in the days of the emperor Constantine, a man named Anthony withdrew into the deserts of

Egypt, where he lived on bread, water, and dates, wore a hair shirt and a sheepskin, and slept on the bare ground. He spent most of his days and nights in prayer. In view of the corruption in the church that followed Constantine's conversion, countless Christians, instead of trying to purify the church, withdrew to pious solitude, following the example of Anthony.

The pious recluses soon organized into groups, or monasteries. In their zeal they renounced personal possessions and marriage. In the centuries of banditry and ignorance that immediately followed the barbarian invasions, the monasteries were a light in the darkness. Monks preserved the ancient learning by copying priceless manuscripts by hand, and, in a world run wild with bloodshed and lawlessness, kept alive the Christian faith and the Christian ideal of self-renunciation.

Though the monasteries produced some of the finest of the popes, and noble spirits like Bernard of Clairvaux, whose hymns we still sing, some of the monasteries themselves in time became seriously corrupt. The oathbound renunciation of marriage often produced evils. Though the monks individually were poor, some of the monastic institutions themselves were wealthy, supporting the inmates in idleness and self-indulgence. Before the end of the Middle Ages, there were monasteries, originally founded in the spirit of earnest piety, that had become a public scandal. Their history suggests that the Christian's life should be in the world, though not of it.

Christian Worship. The earliest worship of the Christians seems to have been very simple. Justin Martyr, in the second century, tells us that they met on Sunday, heard a reading from the Old Testament or a Gospel, followed by a sermon. Then they rose for prayer, after which the Communion was celebrated. Hymns were sung to Christ as to God.

With the passing of time simple things become more complex. So it was with Christian worship. After the era of persecution ended, a halo gathered around the heads of the Christian martyrs. Their very bones—called relics—were said to possess miraculous healing powers. Their prayers were thought to be more efficacious than the prayers of living Christians. Mary, the mother of Jesus, was honored as the chief of these "saints." Then, too, Christians sought to make their faith more vivid by the use of pictures and images of Christ and of the saints. They even addressed prayers to Mary and the saints, frequently while facing holy pictures and images, until some critics began to wonder whether Christianity was sinking to the level of the pagan idolatry which it had displaced. In the celebration of the Communion the idea gradually arose that God, at a certain moment, miraculously transformed the bread and wine into the actual body and blood of Christ, though these still retained the outward appearance and taste of mere bread and wine. Unscrupulous priests sometimes used this belief as a means of demanding exorbitant fees for themselves. In the later centuries of the Middle Ages, great cathedrals, usually with their ground plan in the form of a cross, rose all over Europe. Many of these still stand as noble monuments to medieval piety.

The Crusades. The Crusades were a strange, bloody interpretation of Christianity. When, in the eleventh century, the Turks conquered the Holy Land and insulted and enslaved the Christian pilgrims who were journeying there, the pope, powerfully supported by a strange popular orator named Peter the Hermit, urged that the Christians of Europe rescue the holy places. The First Crusade was the most successful, and captured Jerusalem within three years. The Third Crusade was the most colorful, being led by Frederick of Germany, Philip Augustus of France, and Richard I of England, the last names familiar to all readers of Sir Walter Scott's *Ivanhoe.* There were seven Crusades, and even a Children's Crusade, with children from France and Germany dying in the cold of the Alps, or lost at sea, or sold to slave dealers.

The Crusades were a pathetically misdirected form of Christian zeal, but indirectly they had a very stimulating effect on Europe. Men from different countries mingled in the crusaders' camps, and national patriotism was developed. The travel to distant parts of the world and contact with strange men and customs had their broadening effect on thousands. The last of the Crusades, in the thirteenth century, found Palestine once more in the hands of the Muslims, but it found Europe about to leave the Middle Ages and enter gradually into the altered atmosphere of modern times.

The Corruption of the Church. It is the noblest things that are capable of the most serious degradation. Both the Old Testament and the New, with their Balaams and Caiaphases, warn that even the noblest offices, in unclean hands, can become utterly corrupt.

The Middle Ages—that period between the barbarian conquests and the Renaissance and Reformation—had innumerable noble Christians and brilliant scholars. But as the period drew toward a close it seemed as though the church's power to reform itself had temporarily failed. Many of the monasteries, at first oases in the desert of barbarian invasion, had lost their spiritual vigor. The papacy, once a mighty force against lawlessness and anarchy, and at times a power for reform, had itself become, for the moment, the center of corruption. Such a pope as Alexander VI, of the Borgia family, who was sunk in every kind of vice—covetousness, perfidy, adultery, murder—was not typical of the popes who either preceded him or followed him, but he was typical of his own day. Church worship, once a source of inspiration and strength to Christians, had now become, in large parts of the so-called Christian world, merely a thing of blind superstition and a means of wealth to the higher clergy. Conditions in the church cried aloud for reformation, and the living God was about to answer the need of his people by both a Roman Catholic and a Protestant Reformation. We turn next to view the Protestant Reformation.

2

Two
Great Reformers

Martin **Luther.** God chose a miner's son, Martin Luther (1483–1546), to lead the Protestant Reformation. Young Luther, feeling called by God, became a monk. Though he had always lived an upright life, and though in the monastery he devoted himself to religious ceremonies and activities, he could attain no assurance that God had forgiven his sins. A fellow monk reminded him of the phrase in the Apostles' Creed, "I believe in . . . the forgiveness of sins." Luther read in Paul's epistle, "The righteous shall live by faith" (Rom. 1:17). At last the great truth dawned on him: prolonged fasting, performance of ceremonies, payment of fees to priests and churches, unnatural renunciation of life's wholesome things, even a human being's noblest deeds, are not good enough to earn God's favor. To be pleasing to God, he saw, a man must trust in Jesus Christ with his whole mind and heart and receive by faith God's gift of new life. This truth was soon to have a world-shaking impact.

About this time the pope, who was in need of funds to build St. Peter's Cathedral at Rome, arranged for a sale of "indulgences," by which the purchasers were supposed to be delivered from certain punishments after death. This was too much for Luther, with his newly found knowledge of the way to God by simple faith in Christ. In the year 1517 he nailed to the door of the castle church at Wittenberg—which was often used as a kind of bulletin board—ninety-five "theses," or propositions, attacking the whole system of indulgences. To Luther's own amazement this simple act started the Protestant Reformation, for the response pro and con soon became nationwide.

The pope could not allow such insubordination to pass undisciplined, and sent a "bull," or official order, excommunicating Luther. Luther replied by publicly burning the bull, an act symbolizing his rejection of papal authority. In view of the church's great political and financial power, this required tremendous courage. Would Luther's countrymen stand with him, or with the existing church?

In 1521 the emperor who ruled Germany, Charles V, convened a "diet," or national parliament, at Worms amid great pomp and splendor. Luther was brought before this diet and ordered to recant, or repudiate, the things he had written against the Roman Church. As he stood there before the princes and nobles of the empire, this peasant's son gave the simple answer: "I shall not retract one iota, so Christ help me." Tradition says that he replied further: "Here I stand. I cannot do otherwise. God help me! Amen." Luther had fought and won his battle. He had openly defied church corruption and princely power, and had come away without surrendering a single one of his principles.

On his way home, Luther was seized by armed horsemen and forcibly carried to the Wartburg Castle. Fortunately this was an act of friends to hide him from the possible vengeance of his enemies. While at the Wartburg, Luther translated the New Testament from the original Greek into German, and, a few years after leaving the castle, he translated the Old Testament from the original Hebrew. Laymen could now compare for themselves the new Protestant teachings with the Bible.

The old idea that only an unmarried person can achieve the highest degree of purity and holiness, and that therefore priests should never marry, had sometimes soiled the church with immoralities. Luther declared that a faithful married life is as pleasing to God as virginity, and proved his sincerity by marrying Catherine von Bora when he was forty-two years old.

"Martin Luther . . . is one of the few men of whom it may be said that the history of the world was profoundly altered by his work." He broke the autocratic power of a then tyrannical church, and declared that Christianity is primarily personal trust in God as we know him in Jesus Christ exercised within the context of the Christian church's authority and fellowship. Virtue, he taught, consists in the use and consecration to God of the ordinary relationships and tasks of life, rather than in their renunciation.

Southern Germany remained predominantly Catholic, but Lutheranism became the dominant faith of northern Germany as well as of the Scandinavian countries, Norway, Sweden, and Denmark.

John Calvin. Unfortunately Protestantism was soon divided into two great groups—Lutheran and Reformed. The Lutheran, as the name implies, was led by Martin Luther; the Reformed, or Presbyterian, by John Calvin and others. One regrets that differences of viewpoint on the Lord's Supper and certain other doctrines were permitted to divide the forces of Protestantism, a division that has continued and has greatly increased in diversity to our own day.

John Calvin (1509–1564), a Frenchman born in Noyon, France, was the chief formulator of Presbyterianism. Protestants before him had suggested many of his ideas, and later followers made changes, but Calvin more than any other one man gave to Presbyterianism its distinctive character.

He had originally expected to become a lawyer, and had studied in three leading French universities. When he was twenty-three or twenty-four he was suddenly converted to Protestant Christianity, though he tells us nothing of the details of the experience. Persecution that broke out soon afterward against Protestants in France caused him to flee to Switzerland.

In 1536, in his twenty-seventh year, Calvin published the first edition of his famous *Institutes of the Christian Religion.* It was the best statement of Protestant faith that had yet appeared, and at once marked the young author as a leader of the new movement. In the *Institutes* and in all of his writing, Calvin's main interest was in Jesus Christ as God come in human flesh. God's Truth, he believed, is not wordy speculation, but is Jesus Christ himself. Calvin devoted a large part of his life to explaining the meaning of the Bible, which he tried to understand in relation to Christ. He did not treat the Bible in a mechanical way as a textbook of statements about God, but as a record of God's grace which the Holy Spirit repeatedly causes to come alive for the Christian reader.

Calvin's emphasis on God's grace led him to the doctrine of election—the belief that the Christian is able to choose God only because God has first irresistibly chosen him. The idea, as Calvin held it, is deeply religious, but unprofitable speculations were sometimes drawn from it, especially after Calvin's time. He had much to say about God's sovereignty, that is, his rule over men and over all creation. Calvin had a high view of the organized or "visible" church as our necessary and beloved spiritual "mother." Throughout his life he opposed divisions in the church, and advocated and worked for Christian unity. His religious thought is many-sided, like the Bible after which he patterned it, containing even seeming contradictions held in balance. He was broader in outlook and sympathy than has sometimes been realized, and often deliberately chose a middle view between extremes.

In the same year in which he published his *Institutes,* Calvin was passing through Geneva, Switzerland, intending to spend a single night there. But Farel, a Protestant preacher of the place, told him that God was calling him to remain and labor in this city, and that if he preferred scholarly leisure to the clear voice of duty, the curse of God would rest upon him. Conscience-smitten, Calvin remained to labor in Geneva. Within two years, however, he and Farel were banished from the city for resisting efforts by the civil government to interfere in church matters. But affairs in Geneva suffered from the loss of Calvin's strong leadership, and, invited back, he returned there after three years of exile.

Back once again in Geneva, Calvin developed one of his most distinctive achievements—Presbyterian church government. He provided for four types of church officers: pastors, teachers, elders, and deacons. The clergy were equal, without superior bishops over them, and the lay elders, twelve in number, were elected by the civil magistrates from their own number, to share with the clergy in church government. These principles paralleled the representative civil government that had emerged in such commercial cities as Geneva, and would contribute greatly in later years toward the development of democracy in the Western world.

The ministers met by themselves every week for discussion and every quarter year for self-discipline. Church government for the whole city was exercised by one "consistory" composed of all the ministers and the twelve elders. This consistory performed the function of church discipline. Calvin thought of Christian living as free life in

Christ. "We are not our own, but the Lord's," he said. But Christian freedom for him meant Christlike life as set forth in the Scriptures, not moral laxity. The Geneva consistory undertook to rebuke persons for all sorts of moral or ecclesiastical offenses, and often encouraged the civil government to fine or to imprison them. The whole process was certainly too high-handed for our modern age. But a famous visitor from Scotland, John Knox, seeing the high moral tone of the community, called Geneva "the most perfect school of Christ that ever was in the earth since the days of the apostles."

Calvin had very definite ideas about civil government also. God is God of the state or nation, and the state must be guided by his word. This does not mean that the church has authority over the state; rather, both are directly under God. The state should protect and support a true church, but should not interfere in its internal affairs. Calvin certainly did not teach religious liberty as we know it today, but his resistance to interference by the state in church life did hasten the coming of religious liberty.

Because God has appointed governments, Christians must obey them, Calvin said, except only when they command us to do what is contrary to God's revealed will. In that case Christians must refuse to obey, whatever the penalty. Individual citizens may never revolt even against a wicked government. But a part of the government (like Parliament, for example) may lead a revolt against an evil ruler. By teaching that only God is to be obeyed unconditionally, Calvin contributed greatly, even if unintentionally, to the rise of democracy. Reformed and Presbyterian Christians in France, the Netherlands, Britain, America, and other lands would later go much farther in this direction.

Calvin was interested in the total life of the community. He developed education on both the elementary and the higher level, climaxing in the Geneva Academy, which opened in 1559. He considered learning to be closely related to Christian life. The business life of Geneva too claimed some of his attention. He encouraged the weaving industry. Differing from theologians of the Middle Ages, he recognized the right of moneylenders to charge interest on their loans. More than most church leaders of his day he understood the businessman's viewpoint and needs, but he insisted on the duty of the church to speak out against and to punish economic sins.

Christian worship, for Calvin, receives its distinctive character from the word of God and from the fact that God is entirely spiritual and nonmaterial. Worship is the united act of a disciplined congregation receiving God's word and giving itself to God in praise and obedience. The emphasis is on mind and conscience and away from symbols and appeals to the senses. The singing of psalms amid such solemnity and fervor proved deeply moving. Calvin retained a liturgy for Sunday morning worship, including read prayers along with free prayer. He also prepared liturgical forms for Baptism, Communion, marriage, and the visitation of the sick. Many Presbyterians today who have reacted against the almost slovenly simplicity of nineteenth-century worship have found valuable suggestions regarding worship in Calvin and in the early Reformed churches.

Like all mortals, Calvin was not without serious faults. He was high-strung and irritable, on occasion carried away by uncontrollable temper. His opinions were sometimes ungenerous. He was reserved, but not cold. But his faults were more than overbalanced by virtues more solid than glamorous. His personal life was one of incessant mental toil. While still a university student, he permanently undermined his health by overstudy. Throughout life he was bothered with indigestion and severe headaches. But the resolute mind forced the incompetent body. He rose daily at five or six A.M. His few physical recreations, such as quoits, were brief and infrequent. His time was almost entirely devoted to study, authorship, preaching, consultation, correspondence, and administration. He died at the age of fifty-four, but not before he had completed a magnificent service for the Master, whom he had served so wholeheartedly.

He gave himself and his life to God freely and unreservedly. He took the little town of Geneva and made it a center of influence of the Reformed faith. In its churches and schools, pastors were trained who carried the freedom and truth of the gospel over Europe. Refugees and visitors from England, Scotland, France, Italy, Germany, and the Netherlands came to Geneva, sat at the feet of Calvin for a time, and then returned to their homelands resolved to overthrow church tyranny and to dispel darkness. The tribute paid to Calvin by the Little Council of Geneva shortly after his death was richly deserved: "God gave him a character of great majesty." In the coming chapters we shall watch the growth of the seed that, at the command of God, John Calvin and like-minded leaders had planted and watered.

3

The Presbyterians
on the Continent
of Europe

The Huguenots of France. Within a surprisingly short time after Luther had posted his theses in 1517, the religious issue became the chief concern throughout Europe. The new Protestant doctrines were circulated everywhere by the help of the recently invented printing presses. The question in every country was this: Would men stand by the medieval church or would they follow the Protestant Reformers in leaving it?

France, the near neighbor of Germany and Switzerland, could not ignore the problem. The first Protestant congregation was organized in that land in an unusual way in 1555. La Ferrière, at whose house a group of Christians were meeting, desired his child to be baptized. As there was no minister available, the assembled Christians promptly organized themselves into a little church and elected a pastor, elders, and deacons. The baptism was then administered.

Four years later there were enough Protestant congregations in France to organize the first synod of the French Reformed Church. It adopted a confession of faith drafted by John Calvin, who, from Geneva, guided the destinies of French Protestantism during its early years. This same synod also adopted a book of discipline that laid the foundations for a more fully developed Presbyterianism than that of Geneva itself, with four levels of judicatories: consistories (sessions), colloquies (presbyteries), provincial synods (synods), and a National Synod (General Assembly). This system of ascending courts, found everywhere today in fully developed Presbyterianism, offers the advantage of much local freedom combined with a high degree of central unity.

The remarkable growth of the French Protestants, who were known as Huguenots, aroused the opposition of their religious and political enemies. About sixty were massacred one Sunday as they were going to church in the little town of Vassy. This opened a religious war that, with brief interruptions, tore the country for the next thirty years.

The Synod of Rochelle, at which 2,150 Huguenot churches were reported, was the high-water mark of French Presbyterianism. The next year, 1572, the Huguenots received a terrible blow. The Catholic sister of the king of France was marrying the leading Protestant prince, later known as Henry of Navarre. Catholics and Protestants assembled from far and near to celebrate the wedding that seemed to promise an end to the religious wars. Hardly were the celebrations over when the king's mother, unnerved by the failure of an attempt to assassinate one of the Protestant leaders, persuaded the king to order a general massacre of all Protestants in Paris. This took place on St. Bartholomew's Day, August 24, 1572. The butchery spread over France, until thousands of Huguenots had been slaughtered.

By a strange turn of fortune the political leader of the Protestants, Henry of Navarre, became heir to the throne of France. With the flippant jest that France was worth a Mass, he turned Catholic and was crowned king. Though he had lightly renounced his religion, he did not forget his old Protestant friends, for in 1598 there was issued with his approval the famous Edict of Nantes, granting liberty of worship to Protestants, with a few specified limitations. The edict gave the Huguenots a much-needed breathing spell. From religious wars and other causes, the number of their congregations had been reduced by two thirds in the quarter century preceding the edict.

Henry's grandson, Louis XIV, seeking to unify and centralize the nation, determined to destroy Protestantism in France. In the houses of the Huguenots he quartered soldiers, who treated their hosts with the coarsest brutality. In 1685, he revoked the Edict of Nantes. Thousands of the Huguenots emigrated, many of them skilled workers who, entering England, Holland, Germany, Ireland, and America, permanently enriched these countries with the industrial arts that they took with them.

Many of the persecuted Huguenots fled to the Cévennes Mountains in France, where their boy general, Jean Cavalier, for three years led them successfully against the best troops of France. At last, in 1715, Louis XIV officially declared the "heresy" exterminated; but in that very year the Huguenots, in an old stone quarry near Nîmes, France, were organizing "The Church in the Desert." Within a few years assemblies of 3,000 were not uncommon.

With the coming of the French Revolution in 1789, a great antireligious wave swept France, closing all churches, Catholic and Protestant alike. Six years later the Huguenots were granted freedom to worship God according to their own consciences, a privilege that they have enjoyed from that day to the present. Pastor Bersier, a Presbyterian minister of Paris, spoke truly to the Pan-Presbyterian Council in 1888, when he said: "I represent a great Presbyterian Church—I may say the greatest, when I think of what it has suffered for the cause of Christ and human liberty. And though we are small now, we may say that our poverty has been the riches of many nations." All honor to the heroic Huguenots of France, who so courageously gave up wealth, homeland, and life itself at the call of their Master!

The "Beggars" of the Netherlands. At the time of the Protestant Reformation, modern Holland and Belgium were a single country, known as the Netherlands, ruled by the king of Spain. The Reformation doctrines entered the Netherlands very early, two Protestants being martyred there within six years after the Reformation had started in Germany. It was, however, Calvin and the Reformed, as distinguished from the Lutheran, form of Protestantism that exercised the determining influence on the Netherlands.

In 1555, Philip II of Spain became ruler of the Netherlands. He soon became unpopular there because of his tyranny over the nobles, and because of his persecution of Protestants, a policy that had a damaging effect on the flourishing economic life of the country.

The land was growing restless under this iron rule, and in 1566 five hundred nobles petitioned Philip's regent, the Duchess of Parma, for justice. This formidable paper made the Duchess highly nervous, but one of her counselors, who was standing at her side, sought to hearten her with the words, "Madam, are you afraid of a pack of beggars?" The Protestant leaders proudly assumed the name "Beggars." Failing to secure peaceable redress, bands of Protestants in the same year invaded the old churches, smashed beautiful windows, and broke images, statues, crucifixes, and altars. It cannot be denied that the act was utterly lawless, but King Philip exacted a terrible penalty. The next year he sent the Duke of Alva to the Netherlands with ten thousand troops, who soon executed some eighteen hundred persons.

In this dark hour God raised up a leader for the persecuted people in the person of William the Silent, Prince of Orange. In one of the most desperate struggles in history, extending over a period of forty years, William and his successors succeeded in freeing the northern Netherlands (modern Holland) from the Spanish yoke, gaining thereby the right to worship God according to their own consciences.

In 1574 the tide turned in favor of the Dutch. The Spanish were besieging the city of Leyden. Food was so scarce that cats, dogs, and even rats were eaten. William had courageously broken the dikes, and, after a long delay, the winds brought the waters of the North Sea to the very walls of Leyden. The Dutch ships relieved the city. The grateful population went in a body to the cathedral to pour out their heartfelt thanksgiving to God. William rewarded the fortitude of Leyden by founding a university there a few months later.

Five years after the relief of Leyden the northern provinces of the Netherlands, which were now prevailingly Protestant, formed the Union of Utrecht, from which sprang modern Holland. Within two years this Union declared its independence of Spain. The southern provinces of the Netherlands returned to their allegiance to Spain and to Catholicism. They later became modern Belgium.

William of Orange, against the wishes of the Reformed Church, insisted on tolerating other churches. Thus Holland, which was a great center of trade and banking, became a refuge for people of many lands who were persecuted for their religion. In other nations, too, Reformed and Presbyterian churchmen would later give up their earlier ideal, inherited from the Middle Ages, of imposing their faith by government power and would contribute mightily to the newer and more democratic ideal of religious liberty.

After having successfully resisted persecutions from

without, the Church of the Netherlands was troubled by controversy within. Amid the prosperous business life of the country, some theologians, led by Jacobus Arminius, professor of theology at the new University of Leyden, began to hold views about man's goodness and moral ability that differed from the earlier Reformed emphasis on human sin and God's grace. The whole country became sharply divided, and a synod was convened at Dort in 1618 to settle the dispute. There were twenty-eight delegates from foreign lands, in addition to those from the Netherlands. The synod rejected the doctrines of Arminius, but in endorsing Calvinistic teaching about God's grace made it narrower and more speculative, as often happens in controversy. Before the end of the century, some Reformed Church theologians, reacting against the Synod of Dort, were emphasizing God's love for all men, a tendency that was carried much farther in many lands during the nineteenth and twentieth centuries.

The Church of the Netherlands was a powerful influence in spreading the Presbyterian faith. Huguenots from France, Puritans from England, and Covenanters from Scotland fled from persecution in their homelands and found welcome and shelter in the Netherlands with its religious freedom. As a result of their contact with the churches of this land, they returned home more enthusiastic than ever in their Presbyterian convictions. Dutch colonial expansion during the seventeenth century also had the effect of enlarging the Presbyterian influence of the country. Dutch colonists carried their faith with them to the Dutch Indies, America, and South Africa.

Holland today occupies a high place in the economic and cultural life of the world. Its Reformed churches occupy a distinguished and influential position in the Presbyterian world family of churches.

Presbyterianism Elsewhere on the European Continent. Presbyterianism met with its greatest acceptance in Switzerland, the Netherlands, Britain, and America. We have just discussed France and the Netherlands; we shall view Great Britain and America in later chapters. Here we briefly trace the story of Presbyterianism in some of the other lands of Europe.

In *Germany* the Lutheran, as distinguished from the Reformed, branch of Protestantism dominated from the earliest days, but during the nineteenth century many of the Lutheran and Reformed churches in Germany united to form the Evangelical Church.

In *Bohemia* (Czechoslovakia today), a century before Luther's time John Hus had protested against the corruptions of the medieval church. In the latter part of the sixteenth century many of his spiritual descendants accepted Calvin's views. By the end of the century the Protestants numbered about four fifths of the entire population of Bohemia. But disaster lay just ahead. As a result of their unsuccessful revolt against their Catholic king, persecution arose that reduced their numbers by three fourths. Though toleration came later, Presbyterians have remained a small minority in this land. At the end of World War I, with the erection of Czechoslovakia as a separate nation with universal religious liberty, the future of Presbyterianism in this land appeared more hopeful. But the domination of the land by Communist Russia at the end of World War II made prospects less clear.

In *Hungary* the Lutheran faith, which had entered first, was early replaced by the Reformed, or Calvinistic. By 1600 the Protestants of the country were in a majority, but unusually heavy persecutions that came in the following century cut their numbers by at least a half. As a result of World War I, Hungary lost two thirds of its territory, and after World

War II the land came under Russian domination, but the Reformed faith continues as an important minority movement.

Greece reports some 1,600 Reformed members, and *Yugoslavia* nearly 27,000. *Rumania,* under Russian domination, reports nearly 700,000 Reformed. *Austria, Italy, Spain, Portugal, Belgium,* and *Poland* are prevailingly Catholic countries today. The six together report more than 90,000 Presbyterians.

The present chapter has given a very brief survey of Presbyterianism on the Continent of Europe. It took deep root in Switzerland and in the Netherlands, and flourishes there today; but in other countries of Continental Europe, though it entered some of them early, it proved less dominant. We turn now to the countries that became and still are the principal strongholds of Anglo-Saxon Presbyterianism —Great Britain (especially Scotland and northern Ireland), America, and the former British dominions.

4

The Presbyterians in Scotland and Ireland

Scotland. For more than three hundred years the chief center of Presbyterianism in Europe has been Scotland. The hero of the Reformation in Scotland was John Knox. In one of our first glimpses of his public life, we find him with a company of fellow Christians in the Castle of St. Andrews, which was being besieged by the French. A preacher of this little band, John Rough, "called" Knox to the Christian ministry with these words: "In the name of God, and of his Sone Jesus Christ, and in the name of these that presentlie calles yow by my mouth, I charge yow that ye refuise not this holy vocatioun." Though he fully realized the perils involved, Knox was "not disobedient unto the heavenly vision."

The French captured St. Andrews, and Knox as a prisoner was condemned to row in the French galleys for nineteen months. This was followed by an exile of almost twelve years in England, France, Switzerland, and Germany, with only one brief visit to Scotland.

Knox finally returned to his native land in 1559. When he had left about twelve years before, the Protestants had been only a small minority. Now the whole land was seething with discontent, ripe for reformation. After some fighting, in which valuable assistance was received from Elizabeth I, the Protestant queen of England, the French, who had usurped control of the country, were driven out. The Scottish Parliament which met in 1560 abolished Roman Catholicism, and set up as the religion of the land what soon became fully developed Presbyterianism.

The struggle seemed to be ended, but it was not, for the next year Mary Stuart, the young queen of Scotland, returned to take over the rule of her kingdom after a long sojourn in France. A woman of great personal charm, she was officially committed to the rejected Roman Catholic faith. A contest between two such leaders as Knox and Queen Mary was inevitable. In less than a month after Mary's arrival, Knox thundered from the pulpit of St. Giles' Church, Edinburgh, that one Mass "was more fearful to him then yif ten thousand armed enemyes war landed in any pairte of the Realme." The new queen could not ignore this public challenge to her policies, and summoned Knox to a private interview. On at least five dramatic occasions these two antagonists, the stern reformer and the bewitching queen, stood face-to-face. Knox expressed his opinion of the queen to some friends: "Yf thair be not in hir . . . a proud mynd, a crafty witt, and ane indurat hearte against God and his treuth, my judgment faileth me." Her opinion of Knox, though on different grounds, was every bit as hostile.

To Knox's consternation, the queen seemed gradually to be winning the country back to Catholicism, when a serious moral scandal in her private life brought her into disgrace and necessitated her flight to England, where she was later executed by Queen Elizabeth.

Scottish Presbyterianism, under Knox's leadership, had succeeded in maintaining its existence against Catholic opposition. After Knox's death, under the leadership of Andrew Melville, it faced the further necessity of defending itself against Episcopalianism, the system of government by bishops.

In 1603, James VI of Scotland became king of England also, under the title of James I. From that day to the twentieth century, England and Scotland have been under the same ruler, though for more than a century each country retained its separate Parliament. Intensely autocratic, James bitterly opposed Presbyterianism because of its democratic tendencies, and sought to transform it gradually into Episcopalianism.

Charles I, son and successor of James, carried his father's policy farther. In 1637 he ordered a form of worship, more Catholic than the English Prayer Book, to be introduced into Scotland. When this service was used in St. Giles' Church, Edinburgh, legend says that Janet Geddes picked up the stool on which she was sitting and threw it at the clergyman's head, crying out: "Fause loon, dost thou say Mass at my lug [ear]!" Others threw stools and Bibles. When the bishop sought to quiet the crowd, there were loud cries of, "A pope, a pope, down with him!" Charles, when he heard of the disturbance, was furious, but Scotland was now thoroughly aroused.

The next year great numbers of ministers, nobles, gentry, and peasants gathered in old Greyfriars' Church and agreed to a "National Covenant," pledging to defend the doctrine and discipline of their beloved Church of Scotland. A Scottish General Assembly which met soon afterward rejected all the Episcopalian elements that James and Charles had been introducing, and returned to original Presbyterianism. Charles twice sent an army against Scotland, but twice withdrew, when he found Scottish soldiers ready to resist him.

From this time on, Charles had trouble enough at home. Civil war between him and the English Parliament broke out, and in 1643 the Scottish and English Parliaments agreed to a "Solemn League and Covenant" allying them against the king. Six years later, contrary to the desire of most of the Scots, King Charles was executed. Oliver Cromwell ruled as "Protector," but after Cromwell's death the country restored the monarchy by welcoming back to the throne Charles II, son of the executed Charles I.

Profiting nothing by his father's experience, Charles II at once set himself to transforming Scottish Presbyterianism into Episcopalianism. The Scots were particularly embittered by the fact that some of the king's most zealous agents were former Scottish Presbyterians. Rather than submit to the new regulations, four hundred Scottish pastors and many of their parishioners worshiped outdoors, with some of their own number stationed as armed guards for protection. On several occasions the king's soldiers attacked bands of armed civilians, usually defeating them.

The most uncompromising resisters of Charles II were the so-called Covenanters, who charged that Charles was a usurper for violating the National Covenant and the Solemn League and Covenant which they regarded as covenants with God and as social contracts that constituted the foundation of the government of Scotland. In thus declaring open war against the king, the Covenanters became a heroic but dwindling remnant.

In the midst of this struggle Charles II died, and was succeeded by his Roman Catholic brother, James II. The English Parliament, fearing lest James would reintroduce Roman Catholicism, invited William of Orange, ruler of the Netherlands, and his wife, Mary, to take the throne of England. This was known as the Glorious Revolution of 1688.

William III had been reared in the Reformed (Presbyterian) Church of the Netherlands and was therefore sympathetic to the Presbyterian ideals of his new Scottish subjects. A year after the Revolution the Scottish Parliament declared Presbyterianism to be the official religion of Scotland. "Lay patronage"—whereby certain wealthy laymen appointed the pastors for the various churches, often forcing unworthy men on congregations—was abolished. But the Covenanters refused to be a part of the official Presbyterian Church because the new monarchs had not reaffirmed the Covenants, which the Covenanters considered permanent and which, they felt, should be "renewed," that is, reaffirmed, from time to time. In 1876 most of them united with the Free Church of Scotland.

Shortly after William's death, lay patronage was again forced on the Scottish Church. As a result of this and other causes, some who became known as the Seceders or Secession Church withdrew in 1733 to form the Associate Presbytery. Like the Covenanters before them, the Seceders emphasized "renewing the Covenants," but in a way that was spiritual and nonpolitical—a kind of individual and group rededication to Christian faith and life. This practice of covenanting contributed much to the spiritual life of the early Seceders. In 1847 the Secession Church and the Relief Church, which had also withdrawn because of lay patronage, came together to form the United Presbyterian Church of Scotland. This union was a landmark, because from about that time Presbyterians all over the world became much more active in uniting than in dividing.

But, unhappily, the old grievance of lay patronage was to cause still further division in the Scottish Church. In the great Disruption of 1843, Dr. Thomas Chalmers and other notable ministers led out of the Church of Scotland over a third of its ministers and elders and all but one of its missionaries. The new organization was called the Free Church of Scotland. It was a courageous act, for those who went out automatically sacrificed their share of the financial support which the government gave the established Church of Scotland. In 1874, the old bone of contention, lay patronage, was at last removed, and the congregations of the Church of Scotland also were granted the right to elect their own pastors.

In the year 1900, by an act of enlightened statesmanship, the Free Church of Scotland merged with the United Presbyterian Church of Scotland to form the United Free Church of Scotland. This still left a number of much smaller Presbyterian bodies in the land, but these two—the Church of Scotland and the United Free Church—now constituted the preponderating bulk of Scottish Presbyterianism. In 1929 these two merged under the historic name "Church of Scotland." With more than a million members, this is the largest Presbyterian Church in the British Isles.

Ireland. The people of Ulster, the northern section of Ireland, are commonly known in America as Scotch-Irish, and to the story of Presbyterianism among them we now turn. This is a subject of great interest to every American Presbyterian, in view of the fact that the emigrants from northern Ireland have deeply influenced American Presbyterianism.

Several years before James I came to the throne of England a powerful rebellion broke out in Ulster. The rebels were defeated, and their lands were declared forfeited to the crown. When James I, who had become king of England in 1603, invited colonists from Scotland and England to settle these confiscated lands, the Scots responded so enthusiastically that very soon the population of northern Ireland was quite Scottish; hence the name of these people, Scotch-Irish.

The English Church, at this time Episcopalian, enjoyed official supremacy in Ireland, but felt overwhelmed by the deluge of Scottish newcomers, who were a mixture of Presbyterians and many unchurched. Presbyterian ministers from Scotland worked among the new arrivals. A great revival which came soon afterward confirmed the Scotch-Irish in their Presbyterianism, and defeated the original hope of the officials gradually to wean them away from Presbyterianism to Episcopalianism. Charles I, king of England, unsuccessfully endeavored by persecution to destroy Irish Presbyterianism, even imprisoning many and pulling down the homes of others.

As might well be supposed, the native Irish, who were enthusiastic Roman Catholics, resented this unwelcome intrusion of Scottish and English settlers, and rose up in revolt in 1641, massacring many of the Protestant immigrants. Scotland, retaining a parental interest in its sons who had migrated to Ireland, sent 10,000 troops to suppress the insurrection. As the Scotch-Irish Presbyterian ministers and the Episcopal clergy had almost all been either slain or driven out by the rioters, the only clergymen now left in Ulster were the Presbyterian chaplains of the Scottish troops. For soldiers, these Scots were remarkably religious, for each regiment was organized as a church congregation, having over it a session of chaplain and soldier-elders. In 1642 the first presbytery ever formed in Ireland was organized out of these regimental church sessions. Civilian Presbyterian ministers soon were added to the number of army chaplains, and within less than twenty years there were eighty Presbyterian congregations, with some 100,000 members in Ulster.

Charles II, who came to the English throne at the Restoration of the monarchy after Oliver Cromwell's Protectorate, did all in his power to destroy Presbyterianism in Ireland, just as we have observed that he did in Scotland. He sent troops to disperse the Irish synod at Ballymena, and offered Presbyterian ministers the choice of becoming Episcopalians or of being debarred from their pulpits. It was

their faithfulness at this time which saved northern Ireland
for Presbyterianism. Within a few years these ejected ministers were preaching in improvised churches to enthusiastic
audiences.

James II, who succeeded his brother Charles II, was a
Catholic, and therefore had no zeal for making Presbyterians into Episcopalians. Instead, he gave religious freedom
to all non-Episcopalian groups, including both Presbyterians and Roman Catholics. James also replaced Protestant
army officers in Ireland with Roman Catholic.

Probably as a result of James's policy of placing the Irish
army under control of Roman Catholics, a rumor spread
that a massacre of Protestants was being planned. Conse-
quently, when the government troops commanded by Lord
Antrim, a Roman Catholic, sought to enter the city of Derry
in Ulster, the inhabitants, encouraged by the counsel of a
Presbyterian minister named James Gordon, closed the
gates of the city. A desperate siege of more than a hundred
days followed, in which food became so scarce that rats
were eaten. But relief came at last to the gallant defenders,
who had entertained no thought of surrender. Their exploit
is esteemed as one of Ulster's most honored memories.

By the Glorious Revolution of 1688, Parliament de-
throned the Roman Catholic, James II, and chose the Protestant, William of Orange, to succeed him. The Battle of the
Boyne is another celebrated event of Ulster history, for here
William of Orange, leading a Protestant army, decisively
defeated the ousted king, James II, at the head of his loyal
Irish Roman Catholic supporters, and saved Ulster for Protestantism. King William was a Presbyterian at heart, and
under his rule Presbyterianism in northern Ireland flourished.

The persecution of Irish Presbyterians by Charles II
helped to lay solid foundations for Presbyterianism in

America, for many of the persecuted sought refuge in the New World. In 1683, in answer to the request for a minister for the Scotch-Irish immigrants recently settled in America, the Presbytery of Laggan, in Ireland, sent the Rev. Francis Makemie, who has sometimes been called the father of organized American Presbyterianism. In 1729, and for many years thereafter, as a result of further discontent in the homeland, a steady stream of Scotch-Irish flowed to America. The loss to Ireland was great, but the gain to the cause of Presbyterianism in the New World was almost beyond calculation, as will be seen in later chapters.

Just as political persecution was ending for the Irish Presbyterians, following the Glorious Revolution of 1688, internal doctrinal disputes arose. Low views of Christ's divinity, known as Arianism and Unitarianism, spread among the clergy. The conservative Secession Church of Scotland founded a work in Ireland which soon became known as the Secession Synod, and exercised strong influence against the new doctrinal views. The old Irish Church, known as the Synod of Ulster, underwent a conservative reaction at this time too, and required that all candidates for the ministry subscribe the Westminster Confession of Faith. The two principal Presbyterian churches in Ireland—the Synod of Ulster and the Secession Synod—were now at one in conservative faith and united in 1840 under the name "General Assembly of the Presbyterian Church in Ireland."

This combination of denominations laid solid foundations for the strong Irish Presbyterianism of today. In 1840 the Irish Presbyterians started a foreign missionary enterprise. Not until 1892 was instrumental music sanctioned for worship, and non-Biblical hymns were not permitted until 1895.

One friendly commentator has said of this church: "It may be safely said that the Presbyterian Church of Ireland

is one of the most thoroughly orthodox, consistently conservative, and healthfully active of all the churches in the
great brotherhood of like faith and order." Before we see
what these doughty sons of Erin did for Presbyterianism in
the New World, let us pause to review the story of Presbyterianism in England and Wales.

5

The Presbyterians
in England, Wales,
and the Former British Dominions

England. One of the most creative forces in English history was Puritanism, a movement in which Presbyterians played a very important part. William Tyndale, whose English translation of the New Testament was published in 1525 and who was martyred eleven years later, was an early Puritan.

Meanwhile King Henry VIII, who was not in sympathy with these early Puritan tendencies, in 1534 persuaded the English Parliament to declare the Church of England entirely independent of the pope. But Henry tried to keep the church as close as possible to medieval Catholic beliefs and customs in other respects. Under Henry's son, the boy king Edward VI, many mildly Protestant doctrines and practices were introduced that were to contribute to the Church of England much of its modern Anglican character. Edward's sister, Mary, who succeeded him on the throne, was an enthusiastic Roman Catholic and persecuted Protestants, some of whom fled to Calvin at Geneva and to other Protestant centers on the European continent.

Elizabeth I came to the throne of England in 1558. She was "Protestant" in rejecting the pope's rule over the Church of England; but she was "Catholic" in desiring, though to a less degree than her father, Henry VIII, to retain as much as possible of the medieval Catholic doctrines, ceremonies, and organization.

This did not satisfy the Puritans, however. Many of them, having become acquainted with Reformers on the Continent during their recent exile, had been strengthened in their desire for thoroughgoing Protestantism. Early in Elizabeth's reign the Puritans received their name from their desire to restore what they considered the "purity" of New Testament worship by discarding the Catholic vestments for clergy and Catholic ceremonies. In their zeal for a simplified worship, many Puritans went far beyond the practice of the Reformed Churches of the Continent, and bequeathed to nineteenth-century America a worship service that by then had become quite bare. Most of the Puritans in Elizabeth's day did not intend to leave the Church of England; rather, they desired to remain within it and to carry farther all along the line the revolt against Catholicism, which, they felt, had not gone nearly far enough.

Many, though not all, of the Puritans were Presbyterians; that is, in addition to desiring a simpler form of worship, they felt that the church should be governed by ministers and elders, not by the higher order of clergy known as bishops. In 1572 an *Admonition to Parliament*, advocating definitely Presbyterian principles, was drafted. At about the same time a few skeleton "presbyteries" composed of ministers and laymen tried to function informally within the Church of England. But Queen Elizabeth resisted every alteration. The leader of the Presbyterians, Dr. Thomas Cartwright, had already been removed from his professorship at Cambridge University. An Act of Uniformity prescribed the ritual of worship for every congregation. Many ministers who refused to conform to it were removed from their pulpits or imprisoned. It is estimated that during Elizabeth's reign a third of the English clergy suffered penalties of one kind or other.

Elizabeth died in 1603 and James VI of Scotland succeeded her as James I of England. At a conference the next year James dismayed the Puritans by declaring that a Scottish presbytery "agreeth as well with a monarchy as God and the devil." After hearing the Puritans further, James said, "If this be all your party have to say, I will make them conform, or I will harry them out of the land." True to his threat, James, throughout his reign, made every effort to force Puritans to conform to the semi-Catholic ritual of the English Church.

Charles I carried the persecution of Puritans even farther than did his father, James I. Puritans fleeing from his harsh treatment founded Plymouth Colony and, a little later, Massachusetts Bay Colony in America. Charles's tyrannies of many sorts brought about armed warfare between him and Parliament, resulting in the victory of Parliament's army, led by Oliver Cromwell, and the execution of Charles in 1649.

For a time the Presbyterian wing of the Puritan party dominated the situation. In 1642, Parliament abolished episcopacy and convoked the Westminster Assembly of Divines, which met in 1643, to advise Parliament how to proceed in reconstructing the Church of England. The Westminster Assembly was controlled by men of Presbyterian convictions, and the documents which this body composed —including the Westminster Confession of Faith—are in our own day, with various modifications and supplementations, among the official doctrinal and liturgical standards of the great majority of Presbyterian churches the world over. Presbyterianism seemed to have won completely, for Parliament soon made it the official form of government of the Church of England.

The Westminster Standards were based on the covenant theology which, with variations, Puritans had long held.

God entered into a covenant with fallen human beings, offering them salvation in Christ upon condition of their faith. This covenant theology resembled and strengthened the social contract political thought that the Puritans had inherited from both ancient and more recent times. Men, said the social contract theory, enter into a contract with a king to rule over them. The theory had democratic, even radical implications, for it taught that if the king violated the terms of the contract and became a tyrant, he might be restrained or even deposed. This went far beyond the teaching of Calvin. The social contract view, reinforced by the Puritans' covenant theology, and drawing strength also from more secular sources, was an important foundation for the Puritans' revolt against Charles I, for the Glorious Revolution of 1688, and later still for the American Revolution. Thus Puritanism has made important contributions to the development of democracy in the modern world.

But the victory of the Presbyterians in Parliament soon proved to be more apparent than real. The Puritans were much divided among themselves, ecclesiastically, politically, and socially. They had been able to act together against the king and the Anglicans, but when they came to power their differences caused them to fall apart. A few of the Puritans were satisfied with the episcopal form of church government; many preferred the presbyterian; others preferred the independent, or congregational; the more radical sects desired to weaken church government still further. There were corresponding political differences among the Puritans. Episcopalian, Presbyterian, and some Independent Puritans desired to retain monarchy, but with constitutional controls, whereas some Independents and most of the sects wished to abolish monarchy and set up a republic. Though Parliament was controlled by the Presbyterians, the army was controlled by the Independents and the sects.

And in days of upheaval and change, the real power of the country was in the hands of the army and not of the Parliament. Thus we see the strange fact that, though Presbyterianism had recently been declared by Parliament to be the official religion of England, it never was given a trial on a wide scale in the nation as a whole.

When, after Cromwell's death, the monarchy and Anglicanism were restored in 1660, Presbyterians once more found themselves a persecuted minority. All clergymen were required to become Episcopalians within three months or resign their pastorates. Over two thousand ministers—many of them Presbyterians—gave up their church livings rather than their convictions.

In the Glorious Revolution which occurred in 1688 the political ideals of the Presbyterians and other right-wing Puritans triumphed, because William and Mary, created sovereigns by act of Parliament, would necessarily be, together with their successors, under the control of Parliament. The Toleration Act of 1689 granted toleration to all non-Episcopalian Protestant groups. This was a first decisive step toward the ideal of religious liberty previously held by the more radical Puritans and now being adopted also by the heirs of the moderate Puritans, including the Presbyterians. Thus, though the Puritans had failed to gain control of the Church of England, their political ideals contributed heavily to the transformation of the English-speaking world. Office in the government and education at the leading universities were closed to Dissenters, as the former Puritans were now called, but they became leaders in the business life of England, which expanded vastly in the eighteenth century. By then, however, Dissenters were abandoning the moral restraint on economic sins that Calvin and the early Reformed leaders had tried to provide.

The eighteenth century was an extremely unfortunate

period for English Presbyterianism. At the Revolution of 1688 there had been more than five hundred Presbyterian churches, but a century later only about three hundred. Efforts of Presbyterians and Congregationalists in the 1690's to join forces, known as the Heads of Agreement, did encourage the two groups to cooperate in the American colonies, but these were not effective in England. The civil government abolished the higher Presbyterian judicatories of presbytery and synod. Low views of Christ's divinity, known as Arianism and Unitarianism, were widely held. Another reason for the eighteenth-century decline was an inadequately trained ministry, the leading theological educational institutions being open only to members of the Church of England. Though a remnant survived, much of English Presbyterianism went to pieces at this time. Many joined other non-Anglican churches, especially the Independents, while others became Anglicans, and some abandoned the Christian church entirely. Those who remained under the Presbyterian banner were so decreased in numbers, loose in organization, and vague in beliefs as to be almost negligible as a force in the life of England.

English Presbyterianism was saved by the Scots. Even in the eighteenth century, Presbyterianism in the three northern counties of England had been more successfully maintained than in the rest of the country, due to a steady supply of Scottish-trained ministers for the pulpits and Scottish-born worshipers for the pews. There were also a number of flourishing congregations of Scottish Presbyterians in London. These strong centers had been further strengthened by the Methodist revival under John Wesley.

In the nineteenth century renewed immigration of Scots into England further resuscitated English Presbyterianism. In 1836 the Church of Scotland organized a synod in England which remained under the control of the Scottish

General Assembly. When the Disruption divided the Scottish Church seven years later, most of its English synod went with the Scottish Free Church. A little later a synod was organized in England under the General Assembly of the United Presbyterian Church of Scotland. In 1876 these two Scottish synods in England united to form the Presbyterian Church of England. Thus once more, thanks to Scottish influence, England had a flourishing, even though small, Presbyterian Church of its own. At the close of the last century this church founded Westminster College at Cambridge University, and in 1921 first organized a General Assembly as its highest court. This church later merged to form the United Reformed Church, with more than 190,000 members.

Wales. Wales, the little land on the west border of England, small as it is, has a vigorous Presbyterian Church.

In 1735 a great religious revival broke out in Wales as a result of the labors of Howell Harris, an Oxford-educated lay evangelist. This was before the Methodist revival movement under Whitefield and Wesley had got under way. Within four years Harris had organized thirty groups, which he called, not churches, but societies. Three years later these societies held their first meeting of the General Association. The powerful preaching of the English revivalist George Whitefield also had an inspiring influence on the Welsh movement soon after it had started.

It was not the intention of these early Welsh leaders to found a new church. The converts attended the meetings of the societies, but received Communion in the Church of England. The Church of England, however, soon showed hostility to the new movement, and attendance at the meetings of the societies was punished with fines and imprisonment. In view of this unfriendly attitude, when the revival

movement needed more workers its only available solution
was to ordain its own ministers. Thus in 1811 was organized
the Calvinistic Methodist Church of Wales.

The new church was quite truly Presbyterian in its form
of government. Over the local societies (corresponding to
Presbyterian congregations) were monthly meetings (corresponding to Presbyterian presbyteries). A few years later
two quarterly associations (corresponding to Presbyterian
synods), one for North Wales and one for South Wales,
were added. Over this, a little later still, was erected a General Assembly for all of Wales. This vigorous Welsh church,
like most of its sister Presbyterian churches, holds to the
theological system associated with the name of John Calvin.
It maintains two colleges, home and foreign missionary enterprises, and evangelistic halls in a number of cities. The
work is thoroughly Welsh, the Welsh language rather than
English being used in a number of the congregations. The
Presbyterian Church of Wales today reports over 100,000
members.

Canada. Let us round out our view of the chief centers
of British Presbyterianism by brief visits to the Commonwealth nations of Canada, Australia, New Zealand, and to
the Republic of South Africa.

In 1713, Great Britain received from France what is now
Nova Scotia, and in 1763 all of Canada. Presbyterianism in
Scotland was at that time much divided, and several frag-
mentary Scottish denominations each founded work in Canada. The result was that by 1845 there were five separate
sects of Presbyterians in the eastern part of Canada, as we
now call the land, and three more in the western part. A
series of mergers in the next twenty-three years reduced the
number to four. Of the four, the Church of Scotland had
one group each in east and west, while the United and Free

Churches had union enterprises in both east and west. In 1875 the four came together to form a single denomination, the Presbyterian Church in Canada.

An unprecedented action was taken when the Presbyterian Church in Canada merged with the Methodist and Congregational Churches in 1925 to form the United Church of Canada. This noble experiment prospered, with a communicant membership today of nearly a million. A large body of the Presbyterians declined to enter the union, and continues under the old name, with a membership of about 172,000.

Australia, New Zealand, and South Africa. The island-continent of Australia has a Presbyterian Church of more than 140,000 members. New Zealand, its neighbor to the southeast, has a Presbyterian Church of more than 86,000. Attempts to merge the Presbyterian, Methodist, and Congregational Churches in these two countries, respectively, have been made.

The Republic of South Africa, originally settled by the Dutch, has flourishing Dutch Reformed churches with an aggregate membership of more than 1,245,000 which are Presbyterian in fact, though not in name. The Presbyterian Church of Southern Africa, properly so called, is of Scottish origin, and numbers some 65,000 members. The native blacks have a separate Bantu Presbyterian Church of South Africa.

It is encouraging to see the vigor and activity of Presbyterianism in these newer nations. The rapid development of these lands gives assurance of the further expansion of Presbyterianism as a worldwide force.

Worldwide Presbyterianism. The following statistics are compiled from the World Alliance of Reformed

Churches (Presbyterian and Congregational), *Membership Statistics: August, 1974* (Mimeographed; Geneva, Switzerland). They give some idea of the relative membership of the Presbyterian and Reformed family of churches in the various areas of the world. Of particular interest is the increasing strength of the Reformed "younger churches" of Africa, Asia, and Latin America. Slightly more than half of the membership listed for Africa is within the Republic of South Africa. Most of the figures included in the totals are for communicant membership. Where these were lacking, the larger figures of baptized membership were used and, on rare occasions, it was necessary to resort to the still larger "census figure." The exact ratio between membership in different areas of the world cannot, therefore, be exactly calculated, but the figures do give a suggestive impression of the way these churches are distributed over the world as a whole. These statistics include also, in every area, churches of the Congregational family, which have similar history and character and with which the Presbyterian and Reformed family have been united in this common World Alliance of Reformed Churches since 1970. The total number of claimed adherents is of course much larger than these figures indicate. The statistics are as follows:

Africa	3,660,699
Asia	4,433,652
Australasia	268,003
Europe	11,710,322
Latin America	356,524
North America	6,570,271
Grand Total	26,999,471

Having now surveyed Presbyterianism in lands abroad, let us turn in the remaining chapters to the absorbing story of Presbyterianism in the United States of America.

6

The Presbytery

Plan of Treatment of American Presbyterianism. Chapters 6 to 10 will deal with the history of the Presbyterian Church in the U.S.A. to the outbreak of the Civil War in 1861. Chapter 11 will treat the history of the Southern Presbyterian Church, which separated from it in 1861. Chapters 12 and 13 will resume the history of the Presbyterian Church in the U.S.A. Chapter 14 will treat the history of the United Presbyterian Church of North America until its union with the Presbyterian Church in the U.S.A., and Chapter 15 will treat the subsequent history of The United Presbyterian Church in the U.S.A. which was formed by that union.

The Southern Colonies. Many of the earliest settlers of the first American colony, Virginia, were Presbyterian Puritans in sympathy, though not separating from the Church of England. But with the dissolving of the Virginia Company in 1624, official policy became unfriendly and some settlers conformed to Anglicanism, while others moved away. Presbyterians early settled in Maryland west and east of Chesapeake Bay. Puritan ministers from New England became pastors of Presbyterian churches in Maryland and Delaware. Presbyterians also settled in Virginia along the Elizabeth, Potomac, James, and Rappahannock rivers, but for a time they were not organized in congregations. In 1692 a Presbyterian congregation near modern Norfolk was the first to be legally recognized in Virginia.

French Huguenots formed a church at Charleston, South Carolina, around 1687. About 1722 a presbytery was organized in South Carolina, but this presbytery came to an end during the American Revolution. The early development of Presbyterianism in the South was delayed by the fact that Anglicanism was eventually established by law in all the Southern colonies. This was especially true of early Virginia, where Anglicanism quite dominated the settlements along the coast and up the tidal rivers. As a result, Presbyterianism attained its first substantial strength in the South in the "back country" of the Piedmont and in the Valley of Virginia.

The New England Colonies. New England was settled by the Pilgrims and other Puritans. The Pilgrims, who landed at Plymouth in 1620, had separated from the Church of England sometime before leaving their native land, and had adopted a form of local church government similar to modern Congregationalism. But the Puritans who came to Massachusetts Bay Colony were predominantly those who had never separated from the Church of England, but who had labored to "purify" it from inside, as we saw in Chapter 5. Even before leaving England, they had favored a congregationalist type of church government. Congregationalism was soon so strong in New England that it was established by the colonial legislatures of Massachusetts, Connecticut, and New Hampshire and came to be known as the "Standing Order."

Cotton Mather, a prominent New England Puritan, estimated that of the 21,000 Puritans coming to New England between 1620 and 1640 more than 4,000 held Presbyterian theories of church government. But many of these were soon carried along by the tide of Congregationalism; and though Scotch-Irish Presbyterians and some Huguenots later entered New England, the Presbyterians there remained a small minority compared with the prevailing Congregationalists. New England Congregationalists, especially those in Connecticut, maintained a cordial attitude toward Presbyterianism, and when these Congregationalists moved into the middle and southern colonies they frequently became Presbyterians.

The Middle Colonies. The middle colonies were the early stronghold of American Presbyterianism. Colonial governments in this region, conquered by England from the Netherlands in 1664, granted religious toleration except for an area in and around New York City. This was an attraction to the Presbyterians who had no New World church establishment of their own. More than sixty years before any permanent presbytery was organized in America, New England Puritans, migrating south to Long Island, organized churches which were, or later became, Presbyterian. In the 1640's churches were organized at Southold and Southampton. At least eight others were founded on Long Island within the next thirty years. Francis Doughty and Richard Denton were among the earliest Presbyterian ministers to labor there. French Huguenots organized a church on Staten Island in 1685.

Francis Doughty moved on to New York City, which was then the Dutch "New Amsterdam," where he ministered to a group of Puritans for five years. England acquired New Amsterdam in 1664, and under the autocratic rule of the early English governors of New York, Presbyterianism did not flourish. The Dutch Reformed Church worshiped in the Dutch language, and was unmolested on Long Island and in New York. It was really the oldest "Presbyterian" church in these parts, but its organization remained separate from that of the Presbyterian Church properly so called. French Huguenots founded churches in New York in 1683 and 1688.

Puritans from Connecticut and Long Island founded Presbyterian churches in New Jersey also. In 1667 they organized a congregation at Newark, in 1668 one at Elizabeth, in 1680 one at Woodbridge, and in 1692 one at Fairfield. It is estimated that by 1700 there were about ten or fifteen Presbyterian churches in New York and New Jersey that were of New England Puritan origin, a very important nucleus for the Presbyterianism that was later to be organized. In 1685, Presbyterian Covenanters arrived in New Jersey, fleeing from the "killing times" in Scotland.

In 1692 a Presbyterian congregation began to meet in Philadelphia in the Barbados Company warehouse. Nine years later Jedediah Andrews, a Harvard graduate, was ordained and installed pastor of the First Presbyterian Church of Philadelphia.

Francis Makemie. Francis Makemie has been called the father of organized American Presbyterianism. Before his time, as we have just seen, Presbyterians were to be found scattered over the colonies in isolated congregations, but without having over them any presbytery, which is essential to the complete functioning of the Presbyterian system. To Makemie goes the credit of organizing the first presbytery, and of setting the infant church—now for the first time truly a corporate church—on its way.

Colonel William Stevens, a member of the Council of Maryland Province, wrote to the Presbytery of Laggan in Ireland in 1680, urging that ministers be sent across the sea to Maryland and Virginia. In response, the Irish presbytery ordained and sent a young Irishman, Francis Makemie, educated in Scotland, who was willing to obey the Macedonian call to America.

With great energy Makemie supported himself by private business enterprise and also preached the gospel. From the Carolinas to New York he fulfilled his ministry. Population was scattered, distances were great, horses were scarce, and roads were either nonexistent or hopelessly poor. The traveler was continually in danger from Indians or white robbers. In Maryland, settlements were usually along the rivers, and up these Makemie patiently made his way, bringing Christian exhortation and cheer to many a forgotten cabin. Perhaps as early as 1683 he organized Presbyterian churches at Rehoboth and Snow Hill, Maryland, and later several others nearby.

The Presbytery. The work for which Francis Makemie is most gratefully remembered was his leadership in organizing the first enduring American presbytery in 1706, correctly known as "The Presbytery" or "The General Presbytery." Two features are particularly noteworthy about its formation. For one thing, it united in the persons of its seven ministers the two quite differing and often conflicting heritages of Puritan Presbyterianism and of Scotch and Scotch-Irish Presbyterianism, anticipating the pluralism, even at times polarity, that was to characterize American Presbyterianism. A second important feature of this first presbytery was that it was organized "from the ground up," not "from the top down," as was the Presbyterianism of Scotland which had been adopted by Parliament and implemented by the General Assembly. In America, on the contrary, the higher judicatories were created by the lower, establishing the more democratic nature of American Presbyterianism, and strengthening the concept that undelegated powers remain in the presbyteries, not in the higher judicatories.

American Presbyterianism inherits from Switzerland and Scotland and from the intent of the English Westminster Assembly a tradition of political establishment as a state church. Lingering effects of this tradition perhaps contributed to the desire of American Presbyterians to influence American culture and society with Christian principles in the nineteenth and twentieth centuries. But in America, Presbyterians soon found that in no colony were they a majority and early they became champions of religious liberty. Francis Makemie himself, in a notable legal case in 1707, successfully challenged the right of Governor Cornbury of New York to prevent dissenters from preaching in that colony without a local license.

As originally organized, the Presbytery included congregations only in Maryland, Delaware, and Philadelphia. Some of the Puritan churches of New Jersey and Long Island joined the Presbytery, and new settlers arrived from Scotland and Ireland. The ministers from Philadelphia north to Long Island were mostly of New England Puritan origin; those in Delaware and Maryland, Scottish or Irish. The new Presbytery grew so fast that it soon appeared advisable to organize a General Synod, as we shall see in the next chapter.

7

The General Synod

The **Synod Organized.** Numerically the Presbytery proved to be a great "success." With seventeen ministers on its roll in 1716, the Presbytery transformed itself into a General Synod, having under it the four presbyteries of Long Island (comprising the churches of New York and New Jersey), Philadelphia (comprising the churches of Pennsylvania), New Castle (comprising the churches of Delaware), and Snow Hill (comprising the churches of Maryland). The Synod held its first meeting the next year, but the Presbytery of Snow Hill never came into being as planned.

At its first meeting in 1717 the Synod set apart a "fund for pious uses," with Jedediah Andrews, pastor in Philadelphia, as treasurer. The Synod of Glasgow contributed generously to this sum, and continued liberal financial aid to the infant church for many years.

The General Synod proved to have even more drawing power than the old Presbytery. Jonathan Dickinson, of Elizabethtown (modern Elizabeth), New Jersey, who was to prove himself one of the outstanding Presbyterians of the colonial period, and John Pierson, of Woodbridge, attended the first meeting of Synod. The new Presbytery of Long Island served as a rallying point for the Presbyterian churches of the Long Island region, though most of them did not at once join it.

The Adopting Act. At this time "rationalism" was leading some to try to express Christian truth in such a way that human reason could understand it more completely. As a result, altered views of Christ's deity were being suggested. As a safeguard, British Presbyterians were considering requiring all ministers to subscribe the Westminster Confession of Faith, that is, to declare that it expressed their own beliefs. As the American churches were continually being supplied with ministers educated in Great Britain, the American Presbytery of New Castle requested the General Synod to require all ministers entering the church to subscribe the Westminster Confession. Strenuous opposition to the suggestion was raised by many in the Synod, including the distinguished Jonathan Dickinson. In general, the men of Scottish and Irish origin took the conservative position in favor of subscription to the Confession; and men of New England origin took the more liberal position of opposition to subscription. More than once in its later history the Presbyterian Church was to experience this liberal-conservative polarization.

A split in the church was threatening when the situation was saved by the approval of the Adopting Act, drafted chiefly by Jonathan Dickinson. It provided that every entering minister, or candidate for the ministry, was to declare the Westminster Confession and the Larger and Shorter Catechisms to be "in all the essential and necessary articles, good forms of sound words and systems of Christian doctrine." If there were parts of these standards which any minister could not accept, he should state his "scruples" to the ordaining body and this body would decide whether the scruple was "essential" enough to warrant his exclusion.

Thus the principle was early established that ordaining judicatories had some leeway in the theological interpretation of a minister's subscription, a principle that would prove to be decisively important in later generations. The Adopting Act was passed by the Synod in 1729. The exercise of intelligence and Christian goodwill saved the church from division, without the sacrifice of basic convictions by either party.

Presbyterian Life. Presbyterian church life in the period around 1730 was very different from what it is today. The Lord's Supper was celebrated twice a year, with appropriate sermons preached on the preceding Thursday, Friday, and Saturday. At the Communion service itself the atmosphere was one of deep solemnity. Long tables extended from the pulpit to the door. All those persons who had "tokens" signifying their good standing might partake of the sacred feast.

Church members took their religion seriously. Upon their return home, it was customary for them to discuss the sermon, and often to compare the preacher's doctrines, point for point, with Scripture. The minister's salary was often paid in kind: wheat, Indian corn, hemp, or linen yarn were often specified in his call.

Life was crude, but not illiterate, for the Scotch-Irish immigrants brought along schoolmasters or engaged the local minister to be also the schoolmaster. "It was rare to find [an adult] . . . who could not read and who did not possess a Bible." Parents presenting children for baptism were questioned as to their habits of family worship. The Westminster Shorter Catechism was a staple of spiritual diet, learned at home, recited at school, repeated to the minister. Congregations were divided into "quarters," with one elder particularly responsible for the spiritual welfare of each quarter. The people of a quarter were frequently collected—often in a kitchen or barn—to be catechized by the minister.

The Log College. Because of its Calvinistic emphasis on the word of God, Presbyterianism has always stressed the necessity of a highly educated ministry to expound the word. Quite early, therefore, American Presbyterians became active in establishing means of educating candidates for the ministry. This was soon followed by active promotion of higher education in general.

At first ministers gave theological instruction in their own homes. A somewhat more ambitious venture was the so-called Log College conducted by William Tennent who was pastor at Neshaminy, Pennsylvania. In a little log house, about twenty feet square, Tennent instructed his four notable sons and other men who went forth to play a leading role in the ecclesiastical and educational life of the day. George Whitefield wrote in his *Journal,* "To me it seemed to resemble the school of the old prophets." About eighteen graduated from this institution. Presbyterians of today look back with real pride to this humble but truly great bit of pioneer Presbyterian education.

Though Tennent's Log College closed some years before his death in 1746, the influence of his work kept growing. Academies, similar to Tennent's school, were soon founded at Faggs Manor, Pequea, and West Nottingham. These, as well as later institutions inspired by such early precedents, graduated an amazingly high percentage of ecclesiastical and educational leaders.

The College of New Jersey was chartered in 1746, shortly after the closing of the Log College. Though it was not officially a continuation of the Log College, it did for some time perpetuate its spirit, four of its first twelve trustees

being Log College men. After being briefly located in Elizabethtown and Newark, it moved in 1756 to Princeton and
in 1896 became Princeton University. It has well been called
a "mother of colleges," and, during the days of its predomi-
natingly Presbyterian character, it constituted one more evidence of the effective interest Presbyterians have had in
education since colonial days.

The Great Awakening. Church life in this period was
serious, even to the point of severity, but we shall err greatly
if we look back too wistfully to the "good old days." In 1733
the General Synod expressed concern over the decline of
piety, and urged ministers to pay special attention to pastoral visitation and to the encouragement of family and private worship. The proportion of the population who were
church members was far smaller than it is today. Outside of
New England perhaps not more than one person in twenty
was a member of a church. Even in Puritan New England,
the percentage of church members was surprisingly low.
Grandchildren of the devout Puritan and Scotch-Irish settlers were often quite irreligious. Apprehensive preachers
spoke of the menace of barbarism. But a day of new zeal in
American Christianity was about to dawn.

In the late 1720's, Jacob Frelinghuysen, pastor of the
Dutch Reformed Church at Raritan, New Jersey, was insist-
ing on the necessity of conversion and visible evidences of
new spiritual life in professing Christians. His influence
extended to a young Presbyterian pastor, Gilbert Tennent,
son of William Tennent, founder of the famous Log College
at Neshaminy, Pennsylvania. Gilbert Tennent, who was
located at New Brunswick, New Jersey, a few miles from
Frelinghuysen's parish, began, in 1728, with very evident
success, to preach the necessity of conversion and new
life. Jonathan Dickinson, at Elizabethtown, and many

other ministers caught the revival spirit.

This "Great Awakening" was not confined to the middle colonies, or to any one denomination. In 1734, Jonathan Edwards, Congregational minister at Northampton, Massachusetts, began to preach with life-changing power. During the first year more than three hundred in his community professed conversion. Within six years the revival was quite general throughout New England. In a two-year period, between 25,000 and 50,000 members were added to the New England churches out of a total population of only about 300,000. At Enfield, Connecticut, Edwards preached so graphic a sermon on "Sinners in the Hands of an Angry God" that several times he had to pause for quiet, for all over the building men and women were crying aloud in their distress, feeling that they were slipping into hell.

George Whitefield, son of an English tavern keeper, graduate of Oxford, friend of the Wesleys, and most popular English preacher of his generation, made many trips from England to the American colonies between 1738 and 1770. He traveled from Georgia to New England, giving a unity to the Awakening which it had hitherto lacked. "Under the spell of his matchless oratory men wept, women fainted, and hundreds professed conversion."

In spite of its emotional excesses, which occasionally almost produced hysteria, the Great Awakening had a long-lasting influence on America. Hitherto Christianity in the colonies had been a rather austere enterprise for the spiritually select; now the gospel came home to the common man with power. The Great Awakening decided that America should be a predominantly Christian land. It stimulated moral earnestness, missionary zeal, philanthropy, cooperation across denominational lines, and the founding of educational institutions. It gave new value and confidence to the average man and so contributed to the development of democracy in America. It strengthened the nonestablished churches more than the established, and so helped to prepare for religious freedom. But later revivalism's emphasis on emotion often undermined sober religious thinking, and its almost exclusive interest in individuals greatly weakened the idea of the church.

The Awakening rekindled earlier interest in missions to the Indians. Some of the noblest spirits that modern Christianity has produced are to be found among the early American missionaries to the Indians. One of the most famous of these was David Brainerd, who labored among the Indians from Freehold, New Jersey, to the Susquehanna River. He died a discouraged man in 1747, after only four years of service, but the story of his life, published by Jonathan Edwards, stimulated countless later readers to missionary endeavor both at home and overseas.

The Schism of 1741. One of the less happy by-products of the Great Awakening was the censorious spirit which it developed in some of its chief sponsors. Gilbert Tennent, leader of the revivalistic, or New Side, party, in the Presbytery of New Brunswick, which had been established by the Synod in 1738, was second to none in invective. In 1740, at Nottingham, Pennsylvania, he preached a scathing sermon on "The Danger of an Unconverted Ministry," filled with denunciations of his fellow ministers. Members of the Synod in 1741, after adopting a formal protest against the spirit and practices of Tennent and his party, declared, in a quite irregular way, that the revivalistic New Brunswick Presbytery was no longer a part of the Synod. In 1745 this Presbytery, together with the Presbyteries of New York and New Castle, formed the Synod of New York. Thus the church presented the sad spectacle of being divided into two entirely independent and even hostile bodies, the Synod of Philadelphia and the Synod of New York—the former known as the Old Side and the latter as the New Side—at the very moment when the full strength of a united church was needed for aggressive missionary work along the rapidly developing western frontier.

The Reunion of 1758. Not long after the division, friendly overtures between the two Synods began to be exchanged. Reunion was achieved in 1758, with each side making concessions to the other. The Synod of Philadelphia consented to regard the offensive protest of 1741 as the act of the individual members who signed it, and not as the official act of the Synod. The antirevival group also made the important concession that thereafter candidates for the ministry should be examined as to their "experimental acquaintance with religion." The revival group on its part agreed that irresponsible and unproved denunciations of fellow ministers were to be forbidden; that ministers might not intrude uninvited into the congregations of others; and that greater deference was to be paid to the authority of the church courts. By these and other provisions, the two Synods were reunited in 1758 on the basis of the Westminster Standards under the new name of the Synod of New York and Philadelphia. Here, as on a similar occasion in 1869, the church, by reuniting on a platform of mutual concessions, tacitly acknowledged the futility and unwisdom of having divided.

Growth in the South and West. The 1720's saw the Scotch-Irish, driven by hardships at home, immigrating to the American colonies in increasing numbers. They entered principally at the port of Philadelphia, and by 1732 some of them were moving south into the Valley of Virginia. Many settled in the Valley; some moved east through the Blue Ridge Mountains into the Virginia Piedmont; and others continued along the Valley into North Carolina and beyond. Parts of North Carolina were to become the strongest centers of Presbyterianism in the South. Reflecting the zeal of the Great Awakening, New Side Presbyterian ministers visited settlers on both sides of the mountains. Most notable of these was Samuel Davies, later president of the College of New Jersey, who secured from the Virginia government "licenses" for seven preaching points. In 1755 the New Side Presbytery of Hanover was organized, including most of Virginia and extending far to the south and west. This presbytery in turn was active in missionary work in Virginia, North Carolina, and South Carolina and became a mother of Presbyterianism in the South.

In 1781 the Synod of New York and Philadelphia organized the Presbytery of Redstone in western Pennsylvania. This was the far west of the day. Settlers dressed in deerskins, used blankets for overcoats, and lived in log cabins. Worship was held under the trees or in a fort, no church building having existed before 1790, so far as is known. Often the men came armed, for fear of Indians, and stacked their guns before worshiping, while one of their number stood guard. Wayne's victory over the Indians in 1794 ended the danger. Though material comforts were lacking in these earliest days, many of the pioneers were highly educated men, with deep religious convictions. The ministers shared the hardships, sometimes traveling long distances through forests in their lonely and dangerous service. Often they had to supplement their inadequate salaries by farming or teaching.

It was such a spirit that won the American frontier to

Jesus Christ. We are not surprised that soon the growing Presbyterian Church felt the need of organizing a General Assembly to direct its expanding work. Of this we shall hear in the next chapter.

8

The
General Assembly
Organized

The American Revolution. Presbyterians were second to none in their patriotic devotion to the cause of American independence. Religious as well as economic and political causes underlay the American Revolution. Many non-Anglicans, especially the Presbyterians, were alarmed at the desire of some Americans to secure a resident bishop for the American colonies. Twice in the seventeenth and once in the eighteenth century, this plan had almost been carried into effect. Presbyterians could not forget that many of their immediate ancestors had come to America to escape persecution from government-supported Anglican prelates in England, Scotland, and Ireland. They had no desire to see similar calamities overtake them in their new home, and were ready to resist with the sword if necessary. Congregationalists felt on this issue as did the Presbyterians, and this strengthened the commitment of both groups to the patriotic side in the Revolution.

Many ministers during the Revolution used the social contract theory to justify their revolt against the mother country. As we saw in Chapter 5, some English Puritans had embraced the social contract theory of government which had parallels to their own covenant theology. It was quite natural, therefore, for American Presbyterian ministers to make their pulpits ring with these ideas. Preachers, like secular patriots, repeatedly charged that George III by his "tyranny" had broken his contract with his American subjects and therefore his subjects were released from their allegiance. This was an important contribution to the war effort, for Presbyterian influence in the colonies was great.

May 17, 1775, was a stirring day in the Presbyterian Synod of New York and Philadelphia, meeting in Philadelphia. In the preceding month the first blood of the Revolution had been shed at Lexington. Early in the same month the Second Continental Congress had assembled in Philadelphia. The whole city and country were seething with excitement. In the distraction of these feverish days only twenty-four ministers and five elders were present. The Synod appointed a day of "solemn fasting, humiliation and prayer" to be observed by all its congregations. The Synod also drafted a pastoral letter, which wielded a strong, though restrained influence for the patriot side while still at that early date expressing loyalty to George III himself. This action was the first instance of a pronouncement by the church's highest judicatory on a political or social issue. The practice would increase amid the fervor of evangelical reform in the early nineteenth century, and would expand vastly in the late nineteenth and especially in the twentieth century.

In October, 1776, the Presbytery of Hanover in Virginia endorsed the Declaration of Independence as the document which "we embrace as the Magna Charta of our commonwealth that can never be violated without endangering the grand superstructure it was designed to sustain." Presbyterians individually were also active in support of independence. The most distinguished minister of the Presbyterian Church, Dr. John Witherspoon, president of the College of New Jersey, was a member of the Continental Congress and a signer of the Declaration of Independence.

Charles Thomson, secretary of the Continental Congress, was a Presbyterian elder. Joseph Clark and James F. Armstrong, later Moderators of the Presbyterian General Assembly, were both military officers in the war. Indeed, so universal was the patriotic ardor of the Presbyterian ministers that Dr. Inglis, Tory rector of Trinity Church, New York, wrote in 1776, "I do not know one Presbyterian minister, nor have I been able, after strict inquiry, to hear of any who did not by preaching and every effort in their power promote all the measures of the Continental Congress, however extravagant."

Religious Freedom After the Revolution. We today are inclined to think of complete religious freedom as being characteristic of America. But this did not become the case until after the Revolution. In 1774 nine of the colonies had churches "established," or specially favored, by law. The establishment of Congregationalism was not ended in Connecticut until 1818, and in Massachusetts not until 1833.

Virginia, under the leadership of Thomas Jefferson and James Madison, who were supported by Baptists and Presbyterians, prepared the way for complete religious liberty in the new nation. Jefferson drafted for Virginia "an Act for Establishing Religious Freedom." The Presbytery of Hanover in 1776 had already supported this ideal, declaring: "We ask no ecclesiastical establishment for ourselves; neither can we approve of them when granted to others." Later when a state tax for the benefit of all religious denominations was proposed, a general convention of Virginia Presbyterians took action opposing even this, as did many others; and in 1786 Jefferson's bill for complete religious freedom in Virginia was adopted by the state legislature.

Because of the strength of Presbyterianism, some suspected the Presbyterian Church of the ambition to become established. But, as we have seen, Presbyterians amid the denominational diversity of colonial life had before this become hearty supporters of religious liberty. Therefore the Synod of New York and Philadelphia in 1781 declared: "The Synod do solemnly and publicly declare that they ever have and still do, renounce and abhor the principles of intolerance, and we do believe that every peaceable member of civil society ought to be protected in the full and free exercise of their religion." This splendid declaration voices the best of Presbyterian and American conviction on the subject of religious freedom.

When the religious diversities of the respective states were combined in the new nation, no one denomination had either the numbers or the prestige to hope for national establishment. Thus the way was prepared for the First Amendment to the United States Constitution to guarantee religious liberty, a guarantee that in the twentieth century was applied, by means of the Fourteenth Amendment, to the individual states also.

Organization of the General Assembly. With the winning of the Revolution and the securing of independence, the spirit of patriotic nationalism swept the United States. Many of the denominations, catching this spirit, organized themselves on a national basis at this time. In 1785 the Presbyterian Synod of New York and Philadelphia, also responsive to the new spirit of nationalism, felt that a more adequate national organization for the church would be a General Assembly, constituted of elected delegates and containing synods subordinate to it, rather than the existing Synod composed of all the ministers of the church and an elder from every congregation. Accordingly, the Synod organized a General Assembly in 1788, with the four subordinate synods of New York and New Jersey, Philadelphia,

Virginia, and the Carolinas, including a total of sixteen presbyteries, 177 ministers, 111 probationers, and 419 churches. The church now took as its official name "The Presbyterian Church in the United States of America."

The Synod of 1788 amended the Westminster Confession of Faith and the Larger Catechism to be agreeable to the new American theory of the separation of church and state. The Westminster Directory for the Worship of God was so amended as to become almost a new work. These, together with the Shorter Catechism and a Form of Government and Discipline, the letter of which was specially prepared for the occasion, were to be the standards of the reorganized church. It was further provided that these standards could be amended only with the approval of the presbyteries. As one of the conditions of ordination, ministers were required to answer affirmatively the following question: "Do you sincerely receive and adopt the Confession of Faith of this church, as containing the system of doctrine taught in the Holy Scriptures?" Building on the precedents of the Adopting Act of 1729, presbyteries later increasingly granted leeway in interpreting what beliefs were included in the phrase "system of doctrine."

The first General Assembly met in the Second Presbyterian Church of Philadelphia in May, 1789, with John Witherspoon as its convener. At the very moment when this first Assembly was meeting in Philadelphia, the first United States Congress under the new Constitution was meeting in New York. The Assembly appointed a committee, with John Witherspoon as chairman, to draft an address to President George Washington.

Claims have sometimes been made that the United States Constitution was deliberately patterned after the Presbyterian form of government. It is nearer the truth to say that resemblances existing between the two are due to the fact that the principles of representative government upon which both rest were the common heritage of the men and women of the Revolutionary period, many of whom came of Calvinistic stock and most of whom had been influenced by the political thought of the Puritan revolution.

Further Expansion South and West. Settlers had entered what is now Kentucky and Tennessee before the Revolution, but the ending of the war witnessed a westward thrust from the Valley of Virginia into Kentucky and from Virginia and North Carolina into Tennessee. Settlers pushed on, often by way of the Ohio River, into the lower Midwest, and, encouraged by the Louisiana Purchase of 1803, into the upper Southwest and down to the Gulf of Mexico. The Presbyterians among these settlers were mostly of Scotch-Irish background, as were many others who moved westward across Pennsylvania. Meanwhile other potential Presbyterians of Puritan stock were moving from New England into upstate New York and, a little later, into the upper Midwest.

Another Revival. During and immediately following the American Revolution, Virginia was producing some of the greatest national leaders. Here also two of the most powerful cultural forces of the era met in sharp confrontation— the Enlightenment and deism, espoused by Thomas Jefferson and some other prominent intellectuals; and pietism represented by Baptist and Methodist revivalists. It was amid this stimulating tension that some of the leaders of Virginia Presbyterianism caught the new religious fervor, among them the presidents of Virginia Presbyterianism's two colleges, Hampden-Sydney and Liberty Hall. (The latter became Washington and Lee University.) A new generation of native Virginia leaders of the Presbyterian Church emerged in the revival—Archibald Alexander, John Holt Rice, Moses Hoge, and others. The revival—often called the Second Great Awakening—spread north and west and soon became almost nationwide. James McGready, on a visit to Virginia from North Carolina, caught the revival fire and carried it back to North Carolina and thence to southwestern Kentucky, which in those early days was a typically lawless frontier. Speculation, danger, hard labor, low physical gratifications, quarreling, and fighting were the elements of daily life.

By 1800 the movement had become widespread in Kentucky, and "camp meetings" were being held. These were real camps. Some people slept in tents, others in covered wagons, arranged around a hollow square, where the religious meetings were held. A platform of logs was the pulpit; rows of logs were the seats for the audience. A spectator in 1801 says of a Kentucky camp meeting revival: "At one time I saw at least five hundred swept down in a moment, as if a battery of a thousand guns had been opened upon them; and then immediately followed shrieks and shouts that rent the very heavens. My hair rose upon my head, my whole frame trembled, the blood ran cold in my veins, and I fled for the woods." One historian reminds us that these camp meetings must have been impressive at night. The campfires gleamed, while candles and lanterns hanging from the trees illuminated branches and faces with a dancing glow. To this were added fervent prayers, the chant of the hymns, and enthusiastic exhortations—punctuated by sobs, shrieks, and cries for mercy. Those who came to scoff frequently remained to weep.

This revival was not localized in Kentucky but, in more moderate form, became quite general throughout the nation. It greatly checked the "free thought" and infidelity that had followed the Revolution. Sunday schools now first became widespread in the United States. Home missions, foreign missions, and seminaries and divinity schools for ministerial education developed greatly in the following decades.

The Cumberland Presbyterian Church originated at this time. The Transylvania Presbytery and the Cumberland Presbytery, which grew out of it, ordained men whose education was said to be unsatisfactory, and who rejected part of the Westminster Confession of Faith as teaching "fatalism." As a result of the action of the Presbyterian Synod of Kentucky and of the General Assembly, a majority of the Cumberland Presbytery, in 1810, created an entirely separate denomination, later known as the Cumberland Presbyterian Church. A happy event of the twentieth century was the reunion in 1906 by organic merger of the Presbyterian Church in the United States of America and the majority of the Cumberland Presbyterian Church, by that time grown to be a large and influential denomination.

The Presbyterian Church in 1800. It is in no way derogatory to sister denominations to say that in 1800 the Presbyterian Church was perhaps the most influential single denomination in the country. It had a learned ministry; a sizable membership that was distributed, though not uniformly, over the country as a whole, with many on the rapidly expanding frontiers; an efficient central government supplied by the new General Assembly; prestige from its unquestioned patriotism; and—together with many of the other churches—renewed spiritual vigor from the recent revival. The church was growing rapidly. By 1800 there were twenty-six presbyteries, as compared with sixteen some ten years before. In 1789, the year of the first Assembly, there had been 419 churches, as compared with 511 in 1803.

The greatest task facing the church for many years to come was the evangelization of the frontier. The new General Assembly soon directed all congregations to make annual collections for home missions and to forward them to the Assembly. The church was determined to try to do its part to win America to Christ.

9

The Plan
of Union

The **Benevolent Empire.** The Second Awakening, rapid migration into the West and Southwest, and mercantile contact with non-Christian religions, together with examples from Europe—especially from Britain—stimulated a missionary and reforming zeal that created new problems. How were these new activities to be structured? Should the church itself conduct them or should that be done by interested individuals in nonecclesiastical organizations, each created for a single objective? Protestant churches of the Reformation era were not involved in such activities, and the Presbyterian pattern which emerged in that period made no provision for such functions.

Nonecclesiastical societies would have the double advantage of bringing into cooperation Christian individuals of different denominations and of enlisting only those who were actually interested in the particular society's missionary or reforming objective. But this method would have the decided disadvantage of separating active Christian outreach and reform from the rich Christian heritage of theology and worship embodied in the Christian church, and at the same time would leave the churches to stagnate in a theology and worship that had no contact with the needs of the outside world and no outlet in Christian service.

On the other hand, if the churches were to take over the

new missionary activities and support specific social reforms, the ecclesiastical organizations thus created would
drastically modify the inherited simple four-judicatory pattern of Presbyterian church government. New executive
functions would have to be created which would increasingly alter the inherited polity and would force tacit redefi-
nition of the Presbyterian doctrine of the parity of the
clergy. Furthermore, by conducting such enterprises along
strictly denominational lines, the church would, for some
decades at least, be withdrawing its members from cooperation across denominational lines. The logic of such purely
denominational enterprises would, of course, ultimately
point to the necessity of closer Christian cooperation and
unity between the denominations themselves. An additional
problem, if the denominations were to take over these responsibilities, was that they would impose on all church
members, willy-nilly, a commitment to missionary outreach
and social reform whether or not a member desired to make
such a personal commitment. This problem implied profound theological questions concerning the nature of the
church and the meaning of church membership, questions
that would be explored more fully only in the twentieth
century. But the work had to be done. Christian mission and
social witness were binding obligations on the Christian
conscience. The question was not "whether" but "how."
The church in the early nineteenth century was only beginning to face a problem that would still be very much with
it in the late twentieth century.

Presbyterians in the nineteenth century at first experi-
mented with voluntary societies, but later depended largely
on the church itself to conduct missionary outreach and to
endorse social reforms. The early cooperation in the voluntary societies was made possible by the fact that a dominant
type of Christianity was becoming visible in early nine-

teenth-century America. It had a common heritage in the various branches of English Puritanism and had been further shaped by common American experiences such as frontier life and revivalism. A new American patriotism also was strengthening the forces that were working for Christian cooperation at this time. Thus the stage was set for greater Christian cooperation than Americans had yet attempted, a kind of forerunner of the twentieth-century ecumenical movement. This unity expressed itself in a system of voluntary societies, the so-called Benevolent Empire, closely resembling similar societies organized by Dissenters in England a little earlier. In keeping with the individualistic spirit of revivalism, these societies were conducted by Christian individuals, not by church bodies. They were therefore nondenominational rather than interdenominational.

Some of the societies devoted themselves to missionary and other religious activities; others, organized on the same pattern and often with strong Christian motivation, crusaded for moral reform—against such things as slavery, intemperance, war, Sabbath desecration, dueling, and for women's rights. These societies formed a kind of network, often with interlocking directorates, reaching over a large part of the country, and drawing support from individuals in many denominations, but with their principal leadership supplied by Congregationalists and Presbyterians. Laymen—some of them merchants in international trade —exercised extensive, often controlling, interest in these societies. The influence of this Benevolent Empire on religious and social life was great, tending toward social stabilization and ardent nationalism, sometimes provoking charges of undue thirst for power.

The Plan of Union. Presbyterians and Congregational-ists were at the center of the voluntary society structures. Relations between these two bodies had been close during the colonial period and after. Both inherited Calvinistic doctrines and both used a simple Puritan type of worship. The chief differences were in church government, the Con-gregationalists having no presbyteries with controlling au-thority over the local congregations, but even in this matter the Congregationalists, with a central General Association in each New England state, seemed to be coming somewhat nearer to the Presbyterian practice.

The Second Great Awakening inspired the Presbyterians to send missionaries into the frontiers of central and west-ern New York, where they met missionaries sent by the New England Congregationalists. Would the two churches set up rival organizations in the needy field, or could some method be found of eliminating competition? With a view to solving this problem, Jonathan Edwards, the Younger, when a Presbyterian delegate to the General Association of Connecticut in 1800, suggested a Plan of Union. The next year the Plan was adopted by both the General Association of Connecticut and the General Assembly.

The Plan of Union was an ingenious arrangement mak-ing it possible for congregations to be connected with both the Congregational and the Presbyterian denominations at the same time, and to be served by pastors of either. Presby-terian churches might be represented in the Congrega-tional associations by their elders, while Congregational churches could be represented in the presbyteries by com-mitteemen. Disputed cases might be referred either to pres-bytery or to a special council. The Plan worked so well that in 1808 the Middle Association of Congregationalists in New York State accepted an invitation to become an integral part of the Presbyterian Synod of Albany, without ceasing to be Congregationalists. The Congregationalists, on their part, were so well satisfied with the Plan that for many years they formed no separate organization of ministers in New York State west of the Military Tract.

But, as we shall see, the Plan eventually proved impracticable, being by many derisively dubbed "Presbygational." To have formed an entirely new denomination with a new form of church government that was a cross between Presbyterianism and Congregationalism might have proved feasible. But to have a large group of churches belonging at the same time to two denominations that were distinct and, in important respects, dissimilar, opened the way for difficulties.

Foreign Missions. The first of the national voluntary societies to be organized was the American Board of Commissioners for Foreign Missions, formed in 1810.

In 1806, Samuel J. Mills and a group of fellow students at Williams College gathered near a lonely haystack and solemnly pledged themselves to missionary service. Later most of them entered Andover Seminary, where they were joined by others like-minded. In 1810 some of the men of this group asked the Congregational General Association of Massachusetts to begin foreign missionary activity, and offered themselves as missionaries. The General Association rose to the occasion, and at that same meeting organized the American Board of Commissioners for Foreign Missions, commonly known as the American Board. In February, 1812, five missionaries with their wives sailed for India as the first American missionaries to a foreign land. The American Board also did notable work among the American Indians, particularly in the South, where their Congregational missionaries often joined Presbyterian presbyteries.

By 1879 the influence, direct and indirect, of the little haystack meeting had resulted in the formation of at least five separate foreign missionary boards in America.

In 1811 the American Board invited the Presbyterian General Assembly of the following year to form a similar board of its own to cooperate with them. The Assembly declined, deciding instead to commend the work of the American Board to Presbyterians for their support. The Congregationalists responded to this reply in the same generous spirit in which it had been made, and added a number of Presbyterian ministers and laymen to membership on the American Board.

In the 1830's five Southern synods organized two boards as auxiliary to the American Board. Until the formation of the Presbyterian Board of Foreign Missions in 1838 most of Presbyterian support for foreign missions went to the American Board.

Home Missions. Geography determined that the most important nineteenth-century responsibility of Christianity in America was to be that of winning the West and Southwest to the Christian faith. The nineteenth century was the period when this gigantic task was in large part performed.

In 1803 the Louisiana Purchase more than doubled the original territory of the United States. Five years later the depression caused by Jefferson's embargo policy, enacted the previous year, drove thousands to seek better fortune on the western frontier. Two hundred and thirty-six westbound wagons were counted passing through a village near Pittsburgh in a single day. Western New York witnessed similar sights. Villages sprang up in the West almost overnight. In the single year of 1811, General Harrison's victory over the Indians at Tippecanoe, the beginning of construction of the Cumberland Road, and the launching of the first

Mississippi steamboat all further encouraged migration into the West and Southwest. The Erie Canal, begun in 1816 and completed in 1825, made western New York more accessible. The trek was so rapid that by 1829 nine of the eleven new states were west of the Alleghenies, with six of these Southern or Border. The new states contained more than a third of the population of the entire country. Would the Christian churches be able to rise to this emergency?

None of the churches appeared to be better prepared for the task than the Presbyterian. The Scotch-Irish—Presbyterians by tradition—were scattered along the frontier from New England to the Carolinas and presumably would be particularly amenable to Presbyterian appeals. In 1802 the Presbyterian General Assembly erected a Standing Committee of Missions, consisting of four ministers and three elders. Almost at once fervent appeals for help came from northern, central, and western New York, then from Ohio, Indiana, Kentucky, and Tennessee. By 1811 the work had expanded so much that the Assembly was forced to appeal to the churches for increased aid. In 1816 the Standing Committee's name was changed to the Board of Missions, and it was given greater independence of action though it was still fully subject to the General Assembly.

The spirit of Christian cooperation, so characteristic of this period, found further expression in 1826 in the formation of another of the voluntary societies, namely, the American Home Missionary Society. At first largely Presbyterian in membership, it was soon greatly augmented by the Congregationalists, and proved itself an important agent in organizing and developing new churches under the Presbyterian-Congregational Plan of Union of 1801. The American Home Missionary Society was the first such home missionary organization operating on a national and non-denominational basis, and aided weak churches all over the country. By 1835 this society had 719 agents and missionaries.

But the work was only fairly begun during this period. Samuel J. Mills, of haystack-meeting fame, who had been prevented by ill health from serving in the foreign mission field, investigated mission needs on the western and southwestern American frontier during the years 1812 and 1813. He reported that Ohio, with a population of 330,000, had only forty-nine Presbyterian and Congregational ministers; Indiana Territory, with a population of 25,000, had only one Presbyterian church and minister; and Illinois Territory, with a population of 13,000, had no Presbyterian church or minister at all. Much work still remained to be done.

All honor to these too easily forgotten pioneer missionaries, who labored so faithfully! Over lonely prairie and through virgin forest they rode their circuits, sleeping in rude shanties or beside open campfires. Sexual laxity, gambling, drunkenness were among the conditions that they encountered, and their most earnest efforts were frequently greeted with nothing but indifference or open hostility. Their remuneration was pathetically small—sometimes thirty-three dollars a month, sometimes a dollar a day. Later forty dollars a month was allowed, but not always accepted! One report, for example, tells us that a certain Mr. Chapman "received forty-five dollars and thirty-two cents, traveled two thousand miles, and preached above one hundred sermons." It was the labors of such devoted men as these, in the Presbyterian and other churches, which decided that America, throughout its bounds, was to be a prevailingly Christian land.

Other Activities. The religious vitality and expansive spirit of the times produced many new enterprises. Religious newspapers and journals were founded. The first Presbyterian religious periodical was the *Virginia Religious Magazine,* founded in 1804. Though it survived only three years, it was followed by other more enduring monthly and quarterly journals and weekly religious newspapers in both South and North.

Samuel J. Mills, in his tours of the West and Southwest, had discovered an amazing dearth of Bibles. This stimulated the organization of the American Bible Society in 1816. In 1829 and 1830 this national Bible organization sought to place a Bible in every home in the land. Bibles were also given to immigrants as they entered the country. Another nondenominational agency with missionary outreach was the American Sunday School Union, founded in 1824. Fifteen years later the Union resolved to establish a Sunday school in every western and southwestern community that had none. In 1825 the American Tract Society was founded to publish and distribute religious pamphlets.

Presbyterians were active in all of these nondenominational enterprises. The General Assembly of 1817, in a pastoral letter, showed its sympathy with the prevailing spirit of cooperation: "We are persuaded that all those periods and churches which have been favored with special revivals of religion have been also distinguished by visible union and concert in prayer. We entreat you, brethren, to cherish this union and concert."

Theological Seminaries. The rapidly expanding work of the church contributed to a serious shortage of ministers, but the Presbyterian Church did not yield to the temptation to relax its traditional high standards of ministerial education. Virginia, where the shortage of ministers was particularly acute, led the church in planning specifically for the founding of a theological seminary. In 1806, its Hanover

Presbytery appointed a committee "for obtaining a Theological Library & school at Hampden Sydney College," but it was some years before the plan was consummated. Meanwhile, the General Assembly of 1809 asked the presbyteries which of three possibilities they preferred: (1) one strong seminary in a central location; (2) one seminary for the North and one for the South; (3) one seminary in each synod. The presbyteries favored the first suggestion, and the Assembly organized a seminary at Princeton, New Jersey, which opened with three students in August, 1812. Dr. Archibald Alexander and Dr. Samuel Miller were the first professors, and Dr. Charles Hodge was added to the faculty a few years later.

Other Presbyterian seminaries were founded in this same period: 1818, Auburn; 1823, Union (in Virginia); 1827, Western; 1828, Columbia; 1829, Lane; 1830, McCormick; 1836, Union (in New York). Thus the Presbyterian Church was assured of a more adequate supply of properly trained ministers for its rapidly growing work.

10

One Church
Becomes Four

A **New Period.** Starting about 1830, American life entered a new phase. The spirit of nationalism, awakened by the Revolution, strengthened by the new Federal Constitution, and later by a political "era of good feelings," began to give way to sectional tensions created by growing differences over slavery. The rise to the presidency of Andrew Jackson, with his more radical democracy, brought the "common man" into new power and assertiveness.

This new brand of democracy, together with the spontaneity which revivalism encouraged, stimulated the rise of many new religious movements. The individual believer and his preferences tended to loom larger than the church of which he was a part. Added to this, the heightened sectionalism and the continuing challenge of the Enlightenment to traditional theological views created dissension within many denominations, including the Presbyterian.

Presbyterians and Slavery. The relation of the American churches to slavery offers some suggestive parallels to the relation of the churches to social issues in the twentieth century.

From the 1830's to 1861 the absorbing political question in the nation was slavery. In colonial days there was little protest as the institution gradually expanded. Slaveholding proved unprofitable in New England because of the soil and climate, but this area was the American center of slave trading, a traffic which continued legally until after the Revolution and the profits from which remained as an economic foundation for generations after the traffic itself had been abandoned. In some Northern states, such as New Jersey, slaveholding, with slave galleries in the churches, continued well into the nineteenth century. Meanwhile Northern merchants and Southern planters grew rich from the products of slave labor. No section of the nation was guiltless of this terrible evil.

Eighteenth-century humanitarianism and especially the American Revolution's emphasis on freedom stimulated interest in the emancipation of slaves, but nearly always only at some future date. Moderate antislavery societies became widespread, especially in the South. But there emerged in the early nineteenth century a much more radical abolition movement, some of whose early leaders were exiles from slaveholding states. These exiles contributed heavily toward making southern Ohio a chief center of abolition in the Presbyterian Church. One such exile was a native Englishman, George Bourne, who was ordained by Lexington Presbytery in Virginia. It has been suggested that his flaming denunciations of slavery influenced the fiery abolitionist, William Lloyd Garrison. Another Presbyterian abolition center was upstate New York, led by converts of Charles G. Finney's revivals. The abolition movement, though highly vocal, enlisted only a minority of Presbyterians.

Radical abolitionism soon created an ever-widening breach between those who demanded immediate emancipation and those who now began to defend slavery as a positive good. The moderate position of gradual emancipation, whose concrete accomplishments were meager, rapidly withered. The increasingly sharp divisions over the slavery issue began to appear unsolvable.

Church bodies, like the Presbyterian, that were national in their constituency typically adopted a cautious attitude toward the slavery question. The first official pronouncement on slavery by the Presbyterian Church's highest judicatory was made in 1787 when the moderate ideal of gradual emancipation was emerging: "They [the judicatory] recommend it to all their people to use the most prudent measures, consistent with the interest and state of civil society, in the counties where they live, to procure eventually the final abolition of slavery in America." This action was reaffirmed by five General Assemblies.

In 1818 the General Assembly adopted an unusually strong utterance: "We consider the voluntary enslaving of one part of the human race by another . . . utterly inconsistent with the law of God . . . and . . . totally irreconcilable with the spirit and principles of the gospel of Christ."

After 1832 the discussion of slavery had become so embittered in the nation as a whole that the General Assembly of 1836 voted: "Resolved that this whole subject be indefinitely postponed." The church divided the next year, and its further relation to the slavery issue is seen in the respective attitudes of the two churches that emerged from the division.

From early days some efforts had been made to win the slaves to Christian faith. In Virginia, Samuel Davies and some others had been concerned to bring the gospel to blacks. Sometimes slaves sat in the galleries of white churches, or special services were conducted for them by white ministers. Some masters opposed this work, fearing that it would stimulate the desire for freedom, while others favored it for Christian reasons or because they thought that conversion made slaves more obedient and more productive. Missionary activity increased after the rise of abolitionism. One of the most dedicated missionaries to slaves was Charles C. Jones, a native of Georgia. At various periods in his life he was pastor, seminary professor, missionary to slaves, and board secretary. He wrote a special catechism for slaves, and emphasized the duty of masters to treat their slaves in a humane way, though he did not challenge the institution of slavery itself.

The Presbyterian Church Divides. John Holt Rice was a highly representative Presbyterian of large vision and broad sympathies. A native Virginian, he was the real founder of Union Seminary in Virginia, and declined an invitation to the presidency of Princeton College in order that he might nurture the new seminary. He was keenly aware of the dynamism of the times and of the current restless struggle for power between classes, denominations, and sections of the country. Active in helping to found the American Bible Society, he believed that the evangelical churches must cooperate if America was to fulfill the role of Christian world leadership to which he considered the nation divinely called. He was alarmed at the increasing denominational emphasis which was producing a coolness between Presbyterians and Congregationalists who were the leaders of the Christian cooperative movements. Dr. Rice preached the opening sermons at the General Assemblies of 1810 and of 1820. On both occasions he eloquently warned against the party strife which he saw threatening to divide the church and cripple its mission. His warnings were heard but not heeded, and six years after his death the church divided.

For some years before 1837 there had been those ominous rumblings of controversy between "Old School" and "New School" parties within the church on questions of church government and doctrine against which Dr. Rice had

warned. The Old School, reflecting denominational traditions and interests, became dissatisfied with the Plan of
Union of 1801 with the Congregationalists, charging that
the churches erected under the Plan were not truly Presbyterian at all, and that adequate control and discipline of
them by the church courts was impossible. The Old School
also felt that the Presbyterian Church should have its own
denominational church boards, responsible to the General
Assembly, rather than work in such nondenominational
agencies as the American Education Society and the American Home Missionary Society. On the other hand, the New
School, many members of which were of Congregational
background and training, were quite satisfied with the Plan
of Union and the nondenominational voluntary societies.
They could point to the fact that the Synod of Genesee in
New York State and the two synods adjacent to it, all owing
a large part of their growth to the Plan of Union, contained
more communicant members in 1830 than the whole
church had had in 1800.

The Old School and the New School also disagreed on
certain matters of doctrine. Jonathan Edwards, one of the
leaders of the Great Awakening in the eighteenth century,
had restated—his followers said "improved"—some of the
doctrines of Calvinism. Samuel Hopkins carried innova-
tions farther, and Nathaniel W. Taylor farther yet. So-called
Hopkinsianism and Taylorism were types of doctrine popular in the New School party. These particular theological
issues aroused more interest in the North, where the theological influence of New England was greater than in the
South. But the great majority of Presbyterians in the South
felt much more at home with the theology of the Old School
than with the New England modifications favored by many
in the New School.

Indirectly the slavery issue was also involved in the division. Presbyterians in the slaveholding states constituted less than one eighth of the New School party, but they constituted more than one third of the Old School party. These Presbyterians in the slaveholding states were on the verge of withdrawing from the still undivided church because of continued agitation of the slavery issue at the meetings of the General Assembly. If they did withdraw, it would leave the Northern Old School party in a minority. Now that division appeared to be inevitable, some Northern Old School leaders who were not opposed to slavery preferred to see the church divided along theological rather than along sectional lines and took action to see that this occurred. This would produce a church in which the supremacy of their convictions concerning theology and church government would be assured.

In 1835 some members of the Old School party circulated through the church an "Act and Testimony" over their signatures, warning of "the prevalence of unsound doctrine and laxity in discipline." Securing a majority in the General Assembly of 1837, the Old School men felt that the time for drastic action had arrived. They voted to abrogate the Plan of Union of 1801. They then took action stating that this abrogation was retroactive, and that the four Synods of Western Reserve, Utica, Geneva, and Genesee, organized under the Plan of Union, were no longer a part of the church. This single act removed a large part of the New School party from the church. The one church had now become two separate denominations. This tragic division occurred at the very time when the vast territorial expansion of the nation was about to challenge the church's utmost efforts. On occasion two Presbyterian congregations would be competing in new communities scarcely large enough for one.

The New School Church. The New School party was thrown into confusion by the expulsion of the four synods which were overwhelmingly New School in sympathy and constituted a sizable proportion of the entire party. In the uncertain situation some New School individuals returned to the church, now dominated by the Old School, while some became Congregationalists.

But the vast majority of New School people, though they had not chosen a separate denominational existence, decided to stay together and a distinctive denominational consciousness gradually developed among them. In 1838 commissioners from the presbyteries of the exscinded synods presented their credentials, but were refused seats. Right there they organized themselves as a General Assembly and then adjourned to another building. They were joined by many Presbyterian sympathizers who did not belong to the four excluded synods. Thus the Presbyterian Church presented the strange spectacle of being divided into almost equal denominations, both retaining the original official name ("The Presbyterian Church in the United States of America") yet completely separate and at times even hostile. The two churches during the years of division, 1837 to 1869, were popularly known as New School and Old School. The New School contained about four ninths of the original membership.

This division of the Presbyterian Church in 1837, with its strong influence toward stricter denominationalism, together with the economic depression of the same year, greatly weakened the religious voluntary societies. New School Presbyterians and Congregationalists themselves began to catch more of the spreading denominational spirit. By 1852, New School Presbyterians were beginning to organize their own denominational boards and in the same year Congregationalists held at Albany their first general meeting since 1648 and withdrew from the Plan of Union in which they and Presbyterians had cooperated for nearly half a century.

About half of the New School membership was in New York State, which was one of the chief centers of Presbyterian antislavery sentiment, while less than an eighth of its membership was in the South. The New School General Assembly remained silent on the slavery question for a number of years, but when it pressed the issue in 1853 and again in 1855, its Southern constituency withdrew in 1857 to organize "The United Synod of the Presbyterian Church in the United States of America." The one Presbyterian Church of 1837 was now divided into three—one Old School Church with congregations in both North and South; a New School Church in the North; and this recently formed New School Church in the South.

The Old School Church. Even before the division of the church in 1837, there were Presbyterians who felt that some of the missionaries supported by the nondenominational American Home Missionary Society and some of the ministerial candidates subsidized by the American Educational Society held erroneous theological views. As a remedy, some Presbyterians organized a home missionary society and also an education society, both directly under the control of the General Assembly. The year before the division of the church Dr. Charles Hodge of Princeton Theological Seminary definitively set forth the Old School view that the Christian church itself is a missionary society and should conduct the missionary enterprise directly under its own control. With the decline of the voluntary society system in later years this became the view also of the New School Church and of the later reunited Presbyterian Church. It was a theological expression of the denominationalism that was already becoming quite dominant in America. In 1838, the year after the division, the Old School Church created the Presbyterian Board of Foreign Missions, directly under the control of the General Assembly.

Thus Old School Presbyterians finally decided how they would structure the new missionary and other activities—a problem that their Reformation forefathers never confronted. They would structure these enterprises, not by creating independent voluntary societies, but by inserting the new functions into the system of four ascending judicatories inherited from the Reformation era. This left numerous administrative problems to be worked out, but it did give to the inherited judicatorial system an ultimate control over the new functions.

National Expansion. The period before us, 1837 to 1861, was the era of greatest geographic expansion in American history.

The Republic of Texas became independent of Mexico in 1836 and in accordance with its own wishes was annexed as a state by the United States in 1845. Oregon, which then extended along the Pacific from modern California to Alaska, was claimed in its entirety by both Great Britain and the United States. By a treaty in 1818, renewed in 1827, the two nations agreed temporarily to occupy the region together. In 1835, Dr. Marcus Whitman, a physician of New York, went to Oregon under the American Board. "The [Presbyterian] Church on the Pacific Coast began with the mission work of Marcus Whitman, M.D., in Oregon, and by the organization of the church at Wai-ye-lat-poo (Kamiah) in 1838." In 1846, Great Britain and the United States, by treaty, agreed to divide Oregon between them, with 49° latitude as the boundary. A great territory was thus permanently acquired by the United States. The Treaty of Guadalupe Hidalgo, which ended the Mexican War in 1848, added to the United States an area from which at various times were carved the states of California, Nevada, Utah, Arizona, New Mexico, and parts of Wyoming, Colorado, and Oklahoma. Except for Alaska, this brought the continental United States almost to its present size.

The discovery of gold in California, of other metals in the Rocky Mountain area, and the Homestead Act of 1862 accelerated western settlement. The census of 1790 had shown fewer than 4,000,000 people in the United States; that of 1850 revealed over 23,000,000, of whom more than 10,000,000 lived in the Mississippi basin. Between 1840 and 1869, 5,500,000 immigrants entered America, an increasing proportion of whom were Irish and German Catholics. Many began to talk of the "dangers" of a Catholic West.

The Presbyterian and other Protestant churches were meeting the challenge. It is estimated that between them they sometimes built a thousand churches a year in the Mississippi valley between 1850 and 1860. The achievement of building churches, Christian colleges, and schools; of organizing congregations and installing pastors in these new areas—in a word, the laying of Christian foundations for an entirely new country—all done in a comparatively short time, and supported by purely voluntary contributions, is one of the great achievements of Christian history. The dates of erection of some of the Presbyterian synods of the South and West show that, during this and the following periods, Presbyterians were far from idle in the great task of Christian outreach.

Presbyterian Colleges. The rapid western expansion of the nation, and with it of the church, created a great shortage of ministers on the frontier. But the Presbyterian Church refused to lower its high standards of ministerial education even in the face of the emergency. The result was that Presbyterianism in the new area grew in numbers less rapidly than might otherwise have been the case, but its educational influence was greatly enhanced.

Where there was no schoolmaster in a community, the Presbyterian minister would frequently teach a school of his own, in addition to his parish duties. By the time of the outbreak of the Civil War, Presbyterians had founded forty-nine colleges and universities, located in twenty-one of the then thirty-four states of the Union. This was no small achievement for a single denomination, putting the Presbyterians before the Civil War in first place among the churches as an educational influence.

The Old School Church Divides. On April 12, 1861, Confederate forces bombarded the Federal Fort Sumter in Charleston harbor after President Lincoln started to reinforce it. Northern opinion was rapidly rallying behind the Federal Government; Southern opinion was preparing to support the Confederate government.

In such a tense atmosphere, less than five weeks after the bombardment of Fort Sumter, the Old School General Assembly met in Philadelphia. As the Southern Presbyterians were still a part of the church, many in the Assembly hoped that a political declaration might be avoided. On the third day of the session, Dr. Gardiner Spring, of New York City, moved that a committee be appointed "to inquire into the expediency of making some expression of their devotion to the Union of these States." The motion was tabled. Most of the other denominations had lost their national unity, and many in the Old School Church were anxious to avoid the same fate.

Some days later Dr. Spring again took the initiative, offering resolutions committing the church to the Federal cause. By this time the whole country through the press was taking an interest in the deliberations of the Assembly. Would this influential church lend its moral support to the Union sentiment, rapidly crystallizing in the North, or not? Commissioners in the Assembly were continually receiving telegrams advising them how to vote. In such an atmosphere, and under such pressure of public opinion, the "Spring Resolutions" were adopted after five days of debate, and the Southern commissioners withdrew. The one church of 1837 had now become four—a New School Church and an Old School Church in both North and South. In the following chapter we shall trace the history of Southern Presbyterianism after the separation of 1861.

11

The Southern
Presbyterian Church

The Southern Presbyterian Church Organized.
Even as late as the spring and early summer of 1860 some
hoped that both civil war and division of the Old School
Presbyterian Church could be avoided. Dr. Benjamin M.
Palmer of New Orleans, one of the leading Presbyterian
ministers of the South, in May, 1860, was unanimously
elected by the General Assembly to the Princeton Theological Seminary faculty, an invitation which he declined. Dr.
James H. Thornwell of South Carolina, long a devoted sup-
porter of national unity, during a trip to Europe in the
summer of 1860 even contemplated proposing the gradual
emancipation of the slaves in the hope of preserving the
Union. But when he arrived home he realized that events
had already become irreversible. Soon afterward Abraham
Lincoln was elected President on a platform which was unal-
terably opposed to the extension of slavery. This meant that
Southern territory and power could not be further increased, and that it would be only a matter of time before
Southern institutions would be overwhelmed by Northern
expansion and influence. Rapidly rising public opinion felt
that now or never the South must declare its independence,
if its distinctive institutions and culture were to be preserved. For decades Northern commerce and the beginnings of industry had been creating increasing interdepend-

ence and more centralized government which steadily strengthened federal power and unity, while the agricultural South, ever protective of its distinctive institutions, had long been resisting federal encroachments. The Founding Fathers had never explicitly defined the location of ultimate sovereignty and allegiance, whether it lay in the several states or in the federal government. This constitutional question remained to be decided on the battlefield.

The conviction was widespread in the South that primary allegiance was owed to the state rather than to the federal government. Less than a month after the election of Lincoln, Dr. Thornwell, strong nationalist though he had been, declared that the North by its unfaithfulness to the federal compact had itself dissolved that compact. Less than a week later, Dr. Palmer urged the creation of a new Southern nation. The Synod of South Carolina, though still unwilling to withdraw from the Old School Presbyterian Church, intimated the desirability of secession by the State of South Carolina, an action which that state took on December 20. On February 4, 1861, representatives of seven seceding states, meeting in Montgomery, Alabama, organized the Confederate States of America. Only after the opening of battle at Fort Sumter did the remaining four states of Virginia, Arkansas, North Carolina, and Tennessee join the Confederacy. Virginia's secession on April 17 brought to the Confederacy its capital city and its most venerated military leader, Robert E. Lee. Presbyterian and other church opinion in the South rapidly rallied, and often led, in support of the new Confederacy.

It is an evidence of the strong ties which united the Old School Presbyterian Church across sectional lines that more than a month after hostilities had begun at Fort Sumter, eleven commissioners from three states which had already seceded attended the meeting of the General Assembly in

Philadelphia. The adoption of the Gardiner Spring Resolutions endorsing the federal government supplied the immediate occasion for the organization of a separate Southern Presbyterian Church, but this would undoubtedly have occurred in any case, as Reformed and Presbyterian Churches customarily organize along national lines. On December 4, 1861, commissioners from 47 presbyteries meeting in Augusta, Georgia, organized "The Presbyterian Church in the Confederate States of America." Dr. Benjamin M. Palmer was elected moderator, and Dr. Joseph Wilson, the father of Woodrow Wilson, was elected permanent clerk.

Just as the United States had sought to explain to the world by the Declaration of Independence its reasons for seeking a separate national existence, so the General Assembly of the new Presbyterian Church in the Confederate States of America adopted an address, drafted by James H. Thornwell, "to all the churches of Jesus Christ throughout the earth." Quite in accord with Reformed tradition, the address declared that "two nations, under any circumstances except those of perfect homogeneousness, cannot be united in one church without the rigid exclusion of all civil and secular questions from its halls." All the members of the Assembly in a deeply moving ceremony signed the address individually. The address itself undertook a Biblical defense of slavery as an institution, and subsequent remarks on the floor, unrelated to this address, urged greatly increased religious activity in behalf of the slaves.

The Church's Structure. As previously noted, the rise of missionary outreach and other religious activities in early nineteenth-century America created a change of far-reaching importance in the basic structure of American Presbyterianism. Old School Presbyterians, questioning the theological orthodoxy of the voluntary societies which originated these activities, created church boards to perform the new functions. But some Presbyterians, especially in the South and West, felt that these boards centralized too much power in the hands of a few persons, particularly in the Northeast. The new Presbyterian Church in the South at the outset created four executive committees, instead of boards, the intent being that these committees should have less autonomy than the Northern Presbyterian boards and should leave much more of direct supervision and responsibility in the hands of the General Assembly itself. For many decades executive committees rather than boards continued to be regarded as an important distinction between the Northern and Southern Presbyterian Churches. The four functions assigned to the respective committees were World Missions, Domestic Missions, Publication, and Education. But as the decades passed, these committees acquired increasing responsibilities and came more and more to resemble boards.

For decades before the Civil War, Presbyterians had been discussing not only the propriety and proper functions of church boards but also the office of ruling elder. In nineteenth-century America, with its great expansion of lay activity, it came to be agreed in both North and South that elders should be ordained, which was an American innovation in the office. Should ruling elders participate in the ordination of ministers? Opinions differed, prevailing opinion in the North opposing it, Southern opinion favoring it. Whatever might be its importance, this became a visible difference between the Northern and Southern Churches after the separation of the latter.

Another distinction between the two sectional churches was somewhat subtle, but not altogether unimportant. The Northern Church, visibly paralleling in this regard the greater economic and political centralization of its region, attached greater authority to the respective ascending church judicatories, while the Southern Church, reflecting the more decentralized ideals of its region, left greater autonomy to the lower ecclesiastical levels of congregation and presbytery.

The increasing activism of the American churches in the nineteenth century forced them more and more to stress financial promotion. This was especially important for the newly organized Southern Presbyterian Church. Now an independent entity and fired by a new fervor, its committee on systematic benevolence reported to the General Assembly that much larger gifts to denominational enterprises would be needed and that systematic and regular giving to these causes must be intensively cultivated. The ultimate result was that, some decades after the burdens and losses of the war years, Southern Presbyterians were among the nation's largest per capita donors to church causes.

The Spirituality of the Church. The rise of missionary and reforming activity in the early nineteenth century raised an even more basic question than that of how missionary outreach was to be structured into Presbyterianism's classical system of four ascending judicatories. The more basic question that emerged was: Should the church involve itself in the highly controversial issues of social reform? In colonial times, the Presbyterian Church's highest judicatory made no social or political pronouncements, not even during the colonial wars. But the church's highest judicatory did endorse the patriotic side in the American Revolution. In 1818, the General Assembly, as has been noted, made a strong pronouncement against slavery, but retreated thereafter on this issue for some decades. In 1848, Dr. James H. Thornwell, as a committee chairman, submitted to the Old School General Assembly a recommendation, which that body adopted, that the Assembly not endorse the American Temperance Union, on the grounds that the Christian church is a "spiritual body" and should not thus "unite with" any secular organization, however worthy the organization's objectives might be. But the church's members, said Dr. Thornwell's report, in their individual capacity may properly choose to support worthy social agencies. Dr. Thornwell's report then proceeded to express "affectionate interest in the cause of Temperance" itself. In 1859, speaking on the floor of the still undivided Old School Assembly, Dr. Thornwell asserted even more clearly the doctrine that "the Church is exclusively a spiritual organization. . . . She has nothing to do with the voluntary associations of men for various civil and social purposes that are outside of her pale." Dr. Charles Hodge, writing by way of rebuttal in the same year, took exception to Dr. Thornwell's doctrine and said that when government clearly violates explicit moral injunctions of Scripture the church has the duty of admonishing it. Other Northern Presbyterians, especially in the New School, were already treating even more broadly the church's duty of speaking on social issues, and this long remained an important difference between Northern and Southern Presbyterians.

During the Civil War, the Southern General Assembly and many of its lower judicatories heartily endorsed the Confederate cause, but thereafter the doctrine of the church's "spirituality" was reemphasized and became a protection amid the trials of the Reconstruction era and the desire to restrict relations between the races. By the opening decades of the twentieth century new forces were being felt, and younger leaders in the Southern Church were reconsidering this doctrine. Meanwhile, in Northern Presbyterianism, as industrialization and social complexity stimulated the church to increasing social pronouncements, there was a minority that opposed this trend, but their opposition was not as extensive or as theologically articulate as in the late nineteenth-century South.

Old School–New School Reunion in the South. As previously noted, the Presbyterian Church in 1837 separated into Old School and New School bodies which were almost equal in membership. When the New School Church, the vast majority of whose members resided in the North, pressed the antislavery issue, Southern members of the New School withdrew in 1857 and the next year founded "The United Synod of the Presbyterian Church in the U.S.A.," which after the outbreak of the Civil War became "The United Synod of the South." In 1864, this Southern branch of the New School united with the Presbyterian Church in the Confederate States of America, an Old School body in which it was virtually absorbed. The New School had never had a theological seminary in the South, with the result that the new generation of Southern ministerial candidates after the war studied at the former Old School seminaries in their section. Thus the tradition of New School Presbyterian theology, which had never been widespread in the South, virtually disappeared from that area, whereas it remained a strong living force among Northern Presbyterians.

Thus by 1864 the four churches into which the one Presbyterian Church had been divided were reduced to three— a single reunited, but overwhelmingly Old School Church in the South; an Old School Church in the North; and a New School Church in the North.

The War Years. It was an evidence of the friendly relations that continued within the Old School Church across sectional lines to the very outbreak of military action that

Southern ministers were serving in the North, and Northerners in the South. J. Leighton Wilson, an early missionary to Africa and a secretary of the Presbyterian Board of Foreign Missions in New York from 1853 to 1861, returned to his native South, where for many years after the war he led the Southern Presbyterian Church in a great forward thrust in world missions. Others, too, returned to the South at the outbreak of war, and some traveled in the opposite direction. The oldest son of Dr. Charles Hodge of Princeton Seminary, A. A. Hodge, had married a distinguished Southern lady and was serving a pastorate in the Valley of Virginia, which he continued for a short time after the beginning of hostilities, before leaving for home amid the fond farewells of his parishioners. There were some, too, in both sections who preferred the section of their residence to the section of their birth and remained where they were.

The church's primary spiritual concern during these war years was of course for the soldiers themselves. Some pastors left their congregations for brief ministrations to the army, just as pastors had previously served temporarily on the frontiers; while other ministers were invited by regiments to serve in a more permanent way, without receiving army rank or uniform. Much depended on the support of the higher military officers. General Robert E. Lee and especially General "Stonewall" Jackson, who was a Presbyterian deacon and a deeply devout man, gave hearty encouragement to religious work among their men. A great religious revival swept through the Confederate army.

Not only among chaplains and soldiers in the field but in the churches at home there was deep religious dedication to the Confederate cause. The earliest settlers in Jamestown and New England believed that God had called them to a special destiny. After the American Revolution this sense of providential calling and destiny became interfused with

American national and cultural life as a whole. In the Confederacy this ideal took a distinctive and heightened form amid the struggles of battle and the suffering and loss that followed. This continuing sense of deep religious dedication to an ideal did much to intensify and make permanent the self-consciousness of the South as a region. Professor Ernest Trice Thompson (to whose encyclopedic volumes on *Presbyterians in the South* the present writer is gratefully indebted in this chapter) has rightly written that "only after the Civil War can the South be regarded as the more religious portion of the nation."

The war, which both sides entered reluctantly but optimistically, proved to be an agonizing war of attrition. Under such circumstances, the North, by reason of its much larger population and greater material resources, particularly in manufacturing, slowly prevailed. The South was gradually cut into separated geographical segments amid tremendous devastation of life and property. The struggle ended only·when the heroic defenders and their resources were completely exhausted.

The Breach Between Northern and Southern Presbyterians Widened. On April 14, 1865, five days after the surrender of General Robert E. Lee, President Lincoln was assassinated. The North—exhausted and tense following the long struggle, and hearing entirely erroneous rumors that the assassination was a "Southern" plot—was convulsed with sorrow and anger. The tragedy could not have occurred at a more disastrous moment.

One month after Lincoln's death the Northern Old School General Assembly convened in Pittsburgh. During the war this church had been moving closer to New School hostility toward slavery and to increasingly hearty support of the Federal Government. Throughout the war the Old

School Assembly had retained on its rolls its Southern synods and presbyteries. This Assembly in 1865, instead of forgetting the past and looking toward a new future, declared that to be readmitted each Southern minister must confess the "sin" of secession and renounce the error of considering slavery a divinely sanctioned institution. Church sessions were commanded to apply these same tests for readmission of members to Communion. The Assembly also told its Board of Domestic Missions that the South was now missionary territory. This was one of the most regrettable actions that any General Assembly ever took. It was an example of Presbyterian legalism at its worst. Soldiers on both sides had laid down their arms. Secession and slavery were already buried in hundreds of thousands of graves, north and south. The Confederacy had closely paralleled the objectives and slogans of the American Revolution of which Americans were all so proud. It was unthinkable that Southerners should now be expected to regard as "sin" what they had cherished as the highest of political ideals. This action made an immediate return of Southerners impossible and invited very sharp rejoinders. Later, after both churches had formally withdrawn the bitter things that they had said about each other, increasingly cordial relations gradually developed, but by that time two separate denominational organizations had become fully consolidated.

This harsh attitude of the Northern Assembly in 1865 not only made impossible an early reunion of the Northern and Southern Churches, but even aroused opposition in the Border States of Kentucky, Missouri, and Maryland, which had remained in the Union and in the Northern Church throughout the war. In the autumn of 1865 the Presbytery of Louisville in Kentucky adopted a "Declaration and Testimony" against the antislavery and political pronouncements of the wartime Northern Old School Assemblies, which had climaxed in the 1865 Assembly's demand of repentance for secession and slavery. The Declaration flatly refused to obey such demands. Many in the Synods of Kentucky and Missouri supported the Declaration as did a few in the Synod of Baltimore. The Assembly of 1866 responded by condemning the Declaration and Testimony and forbidding signers to participate in any church judicatory above the level of the session. Finding themselves thus rejected by the General Assembly, signers of the Declaration and others who sympathized with them organized a separate Synod of Kentucky and a separate Synod of Missouri later that same year. In 1867 this withdrawing Synod of Kentucky and in 1873 the withdrawing Synod of Missouri were received into the Southern Presbyterian Church. Thus the action of the Northern Assembly at the end of the war not only rebuffed the Southern Church but cost the loss of a majority of its own constituency in the Border States of Kentucky and Missouri and a portion of its membership in the Synod of Baltimore. But in later years, the fact that both Northern and Southern Churches were operating in these Border States enabled this area to give important leadership in constructive cooperation between Northern and Southern Presbyterians.

The Southern Church Looks to the Future. In December, 1865—seven months after the Northern General Assembly had laid down its impossible conditions for reunion —the Southern General Assembly convened. It was significant that, after extended discussion of various possibilities, the Assembly chose an official name for the church that emphasized its American nationality: "The Presbyterian Church in the United States." Even more significant was a declaration by the Assembly that during the war political allegiance was owed to the Confederacy and its respective states; but now allegiance was owed to the Government of the United States and its states. Thus the church went out of its way to affirm, with no reservations whatever, the national political unity that the ending of the war had restored.

The Southern Church faced great difficulties. The war had left widespread desolation. The South's social structure had been overthrown and much of its physical means of production destroyed. The bulk of its white leadership was disfranchised. For a time the struggle was for physical survival. The church shared fully in the hardships of these days. Many church buildings had been damaged or destroyed. Ministers had left for war service and some did not return. Practically all potential ministerial candidates had been in the army. The church's two theological seminaries—Union Seminary in Virginia and Columbia Seminary in South Carolina—were suffering the common economic deprivation.

But the South gradually began to recover. Reconstruction ended in 1876. The large plantations had disappeared, replaced by many small farms often cultivated by sharecroppers. But by 1880, Southern farmers were producing more cotton than before the war. By then, too, new capital had been accumulated and the South was moving toward industrialization, using its extensive resources of waterpower, coal, iron, and—much later—especially oil. By 1880 many Southern towns had doubled in size, and Texas had the largest population of any Southern state.

The church actively followed the settlers but found, as did Presbyterians in the North, that Methodists and Baptists were growing faster than they, particularly in the rural areas. The strength of Southern Presbyterians was in the towns and cities. In fact, the Southern Presbyterian Church is one of the nation's most urbanized denominations. Some of the increase in population was coming from outside the region, and the Northern Presbyterian Church enrolled members, especially in Florida and Texas, a fact which for a time further strained relations between the two denominations.

Further Development of Structure. As the church grew and times became more prosperous, the General Assembly and its Executive Committees received larger donations and expanded their activities and powers. The church previously had set aside certain Sundays of the year for special offerings for the respective benevolence committees, but the Assemblies of 1910 and 1911 proposed the more efficient plan of an annual benevolence budget, combined with an Every Member Canvass.

Following the successful financial drives of World War I, many denominations launched their own financial "forward movements." This effort among Southern Presbyterians proved increasingly effective in successive years, with the church reaching new peaks of giving. World War II was followed for a time by a new forward thrust. In 1949, in order to handle more effectively its expanding work, the General Assembly transformed its Executive Committees into five Boards—World Missions; Church Extension; Education; Annuities and Relief; and Women's Work. A General Council was given more powers of supervision and was made more representative of the church than had been the Stewardship Committee which it superseded. During the first half of the twentieth century, the membership of the Southern Presbyterian Church almost tripled, but as with many other denominations, the rapid growth of the 1940's and 1950's did not continue into the 1960's.

Southern Presbyterians, early noted for their conservatism, were reluctant to grant official leadership to women, but heartily welcomed their effective financial labors. By 1900 there were about 1,000 local women's societies and some 30 presbyterial organizations, with the first synodical organized four years later. When, by permission of the General Assembly of 1912, a woman was elected as "Superintendent" of the national women's "Auxiliary," the work expanded rapidly. Five years later local circles consisting of small groups of women were created for study and discussion, an effective idea which was widely copied by other denominations. In 1923 the Assembly added three women to each of its Executive Committees and the next year elected a woman as one of its official delegates to the International Conference on Faith and Work to be held in Stockholm. Women were made eligible for ordination to the ministry in 1963.

Foreign Missions. Under the able leadership of Dr. J. Leighton Wilson the church extended its missionary outreach overseas, opening a mission in Hangchow, China, in 1866. Within a decade and a half the church was working in six different countries where forty churches had been organized with some 1,500 converts. Meanwhile women had become active in missionary support, and in 1875 they, together with collections from the church's Sunday schools, supplied one third of the gifts to foreign missions. True to its ideals of decentralization, the church early declared that it did not seek to plant overseas branches of its own ecclesiastical organization, but rather to win converts and encourage them to organize and pastor their own churches.

The church did a notable work in Africa, in the Belgian Congo, sending out as its first missionaries a Southern black, the Rev. William H. Sheppard, and a white. In all, some eleven black missionaries were sent, in a mission that was racially integrated from the beginning. Sheppard and the Rev. William M. Morrison vigorously opposed King Leopold's exploitation of the natives, creating effective pressures in the United States, Britain, and Belgium. Morrison reduced two dialects to writing and began a translation of the Bible, later completed by another missionary. During this period of service the number of converts increased from fewer than 50 to more than 17,000.

The Rev. Hampden C. DuBose, one of the Southern Presbyterian Church's missionaries to China, fought vigorously against the opium traffic there. He organized an Anti-Opium League and distributed literature that attracted international attention, which contributed to the result that in 1906 an imperial edict was issued against the traffic in China. For half a century foreign missions was the church's favorite cause. With the Depression of the 1930's and changes in the international situation, interest in foreign missions was declining among American denominations, but by then Southern Presbyterians had sent out more than a thousand missionaries.

Interdenominational cooperation on the foreign missionary field is widely recognized as a predecessor of the ecumenical movement. In a number of foreign fields Northern and Southern Presbyterians, though unable to unite at home, cooperated effectively. Changing conditions on the field created many problems. What should be the new relation of the sending church and its missions to the increasingly independent younger churches? With what missionary bodies and with what national bodies should the church cooperate? The church, in extensive consultations, made necessary adjustments.

Meanwhile the Board of Domestic Missions of the Southern Church sought to reach non-English-speaking persons at home. Work was done with the extensive Mexican population of the Southwest and with the French in Louisiana, as well as with some of the newer immigrants from the

European continent who were entering the South in the twentieth century.

Worship and Education. The Southern Presbyterian minister was a dignified personage. In the nineteenth century in the pulpits of the older and larger churches he commonly wore a white cravat and black frock coat and, in some instances, even black kid gloves. Sermons were being shortened from an hour or more to forty-five or forty minutes. Revivals, though questioned by some Presbyterians, still flourished, receiving new stimulation in the late 1870's and 1880's from the fame of the Moody-Sankey team.

In the early twentieth century three services a week were customary, but the Sunday evening and Wednesday meetings were already beginning to decline. It was well on into the twentieth century before religious recognition was given to Christmas and Easter, opposition to the Christian Year still surviving. The century saw quartets replaced by congregational choirs, and moderate development of liturgy replacing the earlier almost exclusive emphasis on the sermon.

The church held high its Presbyterian heritage of emphasis on education. In the early twentieth century the Sunday school movement was still expanding, with more careful preparation of materials and teachers. In 1963 the church, constructively influenced by the religious education movement, issued its Covenant Life Curriculum with systematic instruction in the three areas of Bible, church, and Christian life, including social ethics.

The church gradually withdrew from offering primary and secondary general education, but continued to promote higher education. For a time the church cherished the ideal of a college in every synod, or, alternatively, one great

Presbyterian university for the South. While neither of these goals was fully reached, the church had numerous colleges (a few in the Border States maintained jointly with the Northern Presbyterians) that rendered distinguished service.

The Southern Presbyterian Church has four theological seminaries founded on the dates indicated: Union Theological Seminary in Virginia (1823) now in Richmond; Columbia Theological Seminary (1828) now in Decatur, Georgia; Louisville Presbyterian Theological Seminary in Louisville, Kentucky, formed in 1901 by a union of the Northern Presbyterian Danville Theological Seminary (1853) and the Southern Louisville Presbyterian Theological Seminary (1893); Austin Presbyterian Theological Seminary (1902) in Austin, Texas. Louisville Seminary is operated jointly by the Northern and Southern Churches.

Theological and Social Change. The Southern Presbyterian Church, firmly entrenched in its region, with great internal unity and a strong sense of mission to preserve true Presbyterianism, vigorously resisted the winds of theological change that were blowing in the 1880's and 1890's. It rejected a Biblical criticism that questioned the traditional dates and authorship of Biblical books and the historicity of portions of the Bible. It watched apprehensively the struggle taking place on these issues in the Northern Presbyterian Church and efforts in that church to amend the Westminster Confession of Faith. Interestingly, biological evolution attracted far more attention in the Southern Church than it did in the Northern. When Woodrow Wilson's uncle, Dr. James Woodrow, professor of science and religion at Columbia Theological Seminary, came to accept views of divine creation by gradual process, Dr. Woodrow felt that this did not conflict with the Bible, properly understood, or prevent him from affirming heartily the church's Westminster Confession of Faith because he believed that both Bible and Confession were silent on the subject. After prolonged controversy he was removed from his professorship but not from the ministry.

Although a few pastors had earlier voiced mild sympathy for some of the newer theological views, it was not until the 1930's that these became a sharp issue in the church. In 1933 one of the church's leading unofficial papers ran a series of articles challenging Biblical inerrancy and demanding a fresh look at many traditional doctrines. The church and its seminaries were becoming open to quite new ways of thinking. Inevitably these tendencies were resisted by many, and a diversity of thinking such as had not previously existed in the church was emerging.

At the same time that long-held theological views were being challenged, a much wider interest in social questions was coming to the fore in the Southern Presbyterian Church. By the second third of the twentieth century earlier concern about Sabbath observance, alcoholic beverages, and "worldly amusements" had declined and an increasing number of Southern Presbyterians were seeking to involve the church in such crucial issues as problems of capital and labor, war and peace, and race. The race issue was of course the most delicate and the most controversial of all.

In 1936 the Southern Assembly's new Committee on Moral and Social Welfare called attention to the underprivileged position of blacks. The two World Wars in which blacks had fought for the nation, together with the increasing activity of the NAACP and decisions of the civil courts, began to improve the situation of blacks. The Southern Assembly of 1943 declared that all commissioners to the General Assembly should be treated equally regardless of color. The Assembly of 1954 commended, within less than two weeks of its publication, the decision of the United States Supreme Court desegregating public schools. Ten years later the Assembly acted to dissolve its black presbyteries and to distribute their congregations among the white presbyteries. In 1965 the church amended its Directory for Worship by adding the provision that "No one shall be excluded from participation in the Lord's house on the grounds of race, color, or class."

Clearly the church, by its social involvement, was actively revising its long-standing view that the "spirituality" of the church prevented any such activity. The General Assembly in 1935 had explicitly revised the concept of spirituality when it declared: "We believe . . . that the Church in fulfillment of its spiritual function must interpret and present Christ's ideal for the individual and for society. . . . It cannot discharge this part of its responsibility unless it deals with those actual evils in the individual life, and in the social order which threaten man's moral and spiritual development."

North-South Presbyterian Relations. It is interesting to note that intersectional relations of some of the major denominations have differed quite noticeably. The Episcopalians, whose national body meets only once in three years, made no official antislavery pronouncements. During the Civil War the Southern dioceses were retained on the national roll, and at the war's end recriminations were avoided and national unity was quietly and quickly restored. Methodists and Baptists, respectively, divided into Northern and Southern branches over the slavery issue in the 1840's. In 1939 the Methodists reunited. The Southern Baptists, on the other hand, remained separate, but in the twentieth century pushed vigorously into the North, becoming a truly national body, second in size only to the

Roman Catholics. Southern Presbyterians, on their part, remained, far into the twentieth century, a Southern sectional body with clear self-identity, high morale, and—at least until the second third of the twentieth century—with an unusual degree of internal homogeneity.

For more than a century after 1865, problems stood in the way of reunion between Northern and Southern Presbyterians. Most immediate were the harsh actions of the Northern Assembly in 1865. More enduring than this was the fact that the Southern Church, less influenced by theological and social changes that were sweeping other sections of the country, regarded itself as the most authentic representative of true Presbyterianism and the custodian of what was noblest in the Southern heritage. When in the twentieth century the South moved increasingly into the mainstream of American national life and power, and was swept by the same forces of theological and social innovation, differences between the Northern and Southern Churches noticeably decreased. Possibilities of cooperation and even of ultimate union increased proportionately.

The process of renewing relations proceeded very gradually. In 1870 reunion of Old and New School Presbyterians in the North was consummated. In that year and again in 1873 the reunited Assembly attempted to reestablish fraternal relations with the Southern Church, but its attempts to mollify the harsh statements of 1865 were considered inadequate. In 1876 the Southern Assembly took the initiative in addressing the Northern Assembly, but was not satisfied with that body's response. In 1878 the Northern Assembly telegraphed greetings to which the Southerners cordially responded. After greetings had thus been exchanged for the next three years, the Southern Assembly in 1882 telegraphed a formula of reconciliation which it invited its Northern brethren to reciprocate. The statement declared in part: "That while receding from no principle, we do hereby declare our regret for and withdrawal of all expressions of our Assembly which may be regarded as reflecting upon, or offensive to, the General Assembly of the Presbyterian Church in the U.S.A." The Northern Assembly replied, reversing the names and using exactly the same generous words. As a result, an annual exchange of delegates bearing fraternal greetings between the Assemblies commenced the next year.

The year after cordially celebrating together in Philadelphia the centennial of the founding of the original General Assembly, their common ancestor, the two Assemblies appointed committees which recommended closer cooperation in home and foreign missions. The desirability of closer cooperation and comity on the home field was further increased when in 1906 the Northern Church united with the Cumberland Presbyterian Church, thus acquiring many congregations not only in the Border States but also farther south where it had previously been relatively weak.

Notable progress had been made in establishing fraternal relations and increasing cooperation, but actual reunion was still remote. Southern Presbyterians favored the idea of a federation of Presbyterian and Reformed Churches which would leave their church completely autonomous while maintaining advisory relations with the other churches of the Reformed family. In 1914 to protect itself against any hasty unions that might alienate a large segment of its own constituency, the Southern Church amended its Constitution to require a three-fourths vote of all its presbyteries for any church union. Three years later, in response to an invitation from the Northern Church to consider union, the Southern Assembly appointed a committee, but advised the committee to seek federation rather than organic union. After five years these negotiations ended, the Northern

Church holding out for union and the Southern for federation.

Meanwhile the Southern Presbyterian Church was becoming involved in ecumenical relations, where it was often associated with its Northern counterpart. While Southern Presbyterians did not participate in the formation of the Federal Council of Churches in 1908, they joined it soon afterward, and later joined its successor, the National Council of Churches. They became members of the World Council of Churches and of the Consultation on Church Union (COCU) which was seeking union of churches transcending denominational "family" lines. Much of this was in the face of spirited internal opposition, but ecumenical trends prevailed.

In 1954 the Southern Assembly by a vote of 283 to 169 sent to its presbyteries for their decision a plan for a threefold organic union of the Southern Presbyterian Church, the Northern Presbyterian Church, and the United Presbyterian Church of North America. The plan provided that any Southern Presbyterian congregation which did not wish to remain in the union could, by a three-fourths vote of the congregation, withdraw within a year. Debate within the church was intense and emotions were heightened by the recent decision of the U.S. Supreme Court desegregating public schools. The vote of the presbyteries fell far short of the requisite three-fourths majority, 43 opposed and 42 in favor.

But union sentiment did not die. In 1969 the Southern Church amended its Constitution to allow individual presbyteries to belong simultaneously to both the Northern and the Southern Churches. In the same year the Southern Assembly created a new committee to negotiate for organic union with the Northern Church. A plan of union was drafted, but the church decided that before any vote was taken on union, the church should draft and adopt a contemporary Confession of Faith. The draft of such a Confession was accordingly submitted to the presbyteries, but the General Assembly of 1977 reported that less than the required three fourths of the presbyteries had approved it. Under the circumstances this action postponed the question of reunion, but both Assemblies in 1977 took a number of actions to foster closer relations and greater cooperation. Among these actions was a decision to meet simultaneously in the same city in alternate years. With intersectional ties in the nation becoming stronger and closer every year, the ideal of a reunited Presbyterian Church would not die.

Having discussed in the present chapter the history of the Presbyterian Church in the United States from 1861, we turn in the following chapters to the history of the Presbyterian Church in the United States of America since 1861.

12

Reunion in the North

The North and the Civil War. During the Civil War, the Northern churches strained every effort to minister to the spiritual needs of their soldiers. The emergency very definitely fostered an interdenominational spirit, for Christian workers in the armies could not limit their ministrations to fellow sectarians.

In 1861 the Christian Commission was organized in New York, to send preachers, nurses, libraries, religious literature, and comforts to the men at the front. Its work was conducted by "delegates," or volunteer workers, drawn mostly from the churches. Many ministers served in this way for short periods. During the four years of the war, the Commission received more than $2,500,000, contributed largely through the churches. The American Bible Society too was very active, distributing almost a million Bibles and Testaments in a single year, while Tract Societies circulated thousands of tracts in the army.

The period of Reconstruction is an era that few in any section of the country recall today with any satisfaction. A particularly regrettable feature of it, from an ecclesiastical point of view, was the practice of Union armies as they advanced into the South of turning over to the use of Northern denominations and preachers of Northern sympathies the churches which they had taken. At the close of the war, the Northern Presbyterian Church tried, with notable lack of success, to set up churches, presbyteries, and synods composed of persons in the South who would deny that slavery was divinely sanctioned and who would confess the "sin" of secession.

The effects of the Civil War, as of any war, on the moral and spiritual life of the country were injurious. The interest of the churches was, for the time, diverted. In the light of these facts, the era of corruption that overwhelmed the national Government need be considered no surprise. With the period of sectional war and heightened denominational divisiveness at an end, the churches entered into a new era of interdenominational goodwill and expansiveness of spirit and sympathy.

The Reunion. The Civil War was a watershed in American history. The closer unity that it forced upon the states emphasized and strengthened forces already moving toward closer unity in political government, in business organization, and in church life. After the Civil War the West was being settled faster than ever, and Presbyterians realized that they could carry the gospel to the new settlers more effectively if their Old School and New School Churches were to unite. Reunion was aided by the fact that New School Presbyterians had developed a stronger denominational consciousness and now they also conducted their missionary work by denominational boards rather than through the nondenominational voluntary societies. Then, too, theological change was in the air, and Old School Presbyterians were now less inclined to insist on the theological points that distinguished them from the New School. They had also been drawn closer together in their common support of the war. The result was that in 1869, after five years of negotiation, the Old School and the New

School Presbyterian Churches reunited on the basis of the Westminster Standards "pure and simple." The name of the reunited church was the Presbyterian Church in the United States of America—the name before the division and the name that each of the branches held during the division. The reunion of 1869, like the earlier reunion of 1758, underlined the futility and wastefulness of ever having divided. The four churches into which the one "Presbyterian Church in the United States of America" had divided were, by 1869, consolidated into two churches—one reunited in the North and one reunited in the South. This remaining division continued for more than a century.

Evolution and Biblical Criticism. The decades after the Civil War saw great changes in culture and thinking which created disturbing theological problems for the churches. In 1859, Charles Darwin had published his *Origin of Species.* Northern Presbyterians, like other Christians, differed among themselves as to the relation between evolution and the Genesis story of creation, and as to how far ideas of development were to be applied to the understanding of Christianity itself.

In the field of Biblical studies, scholars abroad, especially in Germany, using methods of "higher criticism," had been applying to the Bible the same scholarly analysis that had been applied to other literary and historical writings. They concluded that the Bible contained incorrect statements about history and science and other matters, and that traditional views concerning the authors and dates of Bible books were in many cases erroneous. Prof. Charles A. Briggs, of Union Seminary, New York, considered it crucially important that the new conclusions be accepted and interpreted by evangelical Christians and not become a monopoly of the enemies of historic Christianity. Therefore by articles in the 1880's and especially by an address in 1891 he introduced into the Presbyterian Church animated discussion of the new views.

Dr. Briggs believed deeply that God had revealed himself in the Old and New Testaments and especially in his Son, Jesus Christ, and that the Bible was a sufficiently trustworthy record of this revelation. But the vast majority of Presbyterians at that time believed that a more literal view of the Bible was necessary as a means of defending and expounding the Christian faith. Therefore the General Assembly in 1892 and in 1893 declared that the original manuscripts of the Bible were "without error," and in 1893 suspended Dr. Briggs from the Presbyterian ministry. This effort to suppress Dr. Briggs's views gave them national publicity. Presbyterian seminaries today are open to the most advanced scholarly views of the Bible.

Creedal Revision. In the latter part of the nineteenth century, Christians throughout the world were laying increased emphasis on God's love. Many Calvinists were turning away from some of the older interpretations of predestination. This explains the fact that the General Assembly of 1889 received memorials from fifteen presbyteries asking that the Westminster Confession of Faith be revised. In the discussion that followed, some wanted no change. Others, with more historical awareness, desired to write a new statement of the church's contemporary faith, while leaving the classical Westminster Confession unchanged. The Assembly chose neither of these counsels. Instead, in 1892, it submitted proposed revisions to the presbyteries for their approval, but not one of the proposed revisions was accepted by the required two thirds of the presbyteries of the church. It was frustrating for a majority of the presbyteries to be left desiring what a two-thirds majority would not grant.

Revision was taken up later with greater success. In 1903 the church adopted six amendments to the Confession, including new chapters entitled "Of the Holy Spirit" and "Of the Love of God and Missions," as well as a "Declaratory Statement," which asserted God's love for all mankind and also the salvation of all dying in infancy. While relieving some pressure, these limited amendments failed to give the church a really contemporary expression of its faith. The inevitable result was that the formula of ministerial subscription to the Confession came to be more and more broadly interpreted by ordaining presbyteries. Thus the effort to prevent theological change by resisting restatement had exactly the opposite effect of depriving the church of an agreed-upon norm of its real present faith.

Fundamentalism. Amid extensive changes that were taking place in European and American patterns of thinking, it was becoming increasingly necessary for Christians to state the deepest truths of the gospel in language and in thought forms that would deal creatively with the new ideas, and would at the same time be true to the realities of Christianity. At every new stage of Christian history this restatement of Christian truth has been a necessary though difficult task. In America there was fear that essentials of Christianity were in danger, and in 1909 a series of twelve booklets entitled *The Fundamentals: A Testimony to the Truth* began to be published. The volumes set forth five doctrines as fundamental Christian truths: the virgin birth of Christ, the physical resurrection, the inerrancy of the Scriptures, the substitutionary atonement, and Christ's imminent physical Second Coming. Two wealthy laymen financed the free distribution of 2,500,000 copies.

In the Presbyterian Church there was widespread and often tense discussion of these issues in the church's newspapers and judicatories. The General Assemblies of 1910, 1916, and 1923 set forth five doctrines as "essential doctrines," but the Assembly of 1927, taking a different view of the matter, declared that the Assembly may not, without the joint action of the presbyteries, single out particular doctrines as "essential" and binding on all ministers. Thus the church declined to adopt the platform of so-called fundamentalism. Fundamentalism warned the church of dangers involved in theological change, but the times called for more sympathetic understanding of contemporary thought and social duty and for more profound analysis of the nature of Christianity than was offered by fundamentalism.

The Church's Social Message. During the same decades that the church was struggling with these theological issues, far-reaching social changes were sweeping the country. The industrial revolution, substituting machinery for hand labor, had reached the United States about 1830–1840, but it was after the Civil War that its full effects began to be felt. Workingmen, no longer owning their own tools and not yet organized, were economically helpless. Hours were long, wages low, and working conditions often dangerous and unsanitary. Mass movements to the cities created depressing and crime-breeding slums. Unprecedented numbers of immigrants, now mostly of foreign language and non-Protestant, could not be immediately assimilated. The individual was increasingly helpless in the new interdependent industrial society with its growing centralization of economic and political power. These conditions caught the churches off balance. American Christians, under the influence of political and economic individualism, and under the influence of the frontier and of revivalism, had come to think that the responsibility of the Christian church could properly be confined to "saving the souls" of individuals. But medieval Christians, and the Reformed and Anglican churches, and the early New England Puritans had held the much larger ideal that the Christian church itself has responsibilities to society as a whole as well as to individuals. The new conditions made it morally necessary for the American churches to reassert their larger responsibilities. A corporate Christian approach to the altered social situation was needed.

A Presbyterian businessman, Stephen Colwell, had pioneered in 1854 by writing *New Themes for the Protestant Clergy*, in which he criticized the church for its forgetfulness of Christian love and for its failure to denounce contemporary covetousness as sin. But most writers in Presbyterian and other religious periodicals in the 1880's and 1890's were still inclined to the view that a man should be allowed to run his business as he liked, and to look upon those who pressed for larger rights for workingmen as disturbers of the peace. In 1903, however, the Presbyterian Church created a Workingmen's Department, and sponsored the Labor Temple in New York City. The General Assembly in 1910 offered to industry, in what has sometimes been referred to as a "social creed," a series of moral goals which it clarified and expanded in succeeding years. The church was recovering its heritage and reasserting that the Christian church has the prophetic task of reminding men that whenever human values are involved, there God's will and God's judgment must be faced. An emerging "social gospel" emphasized God's immanence in all areas of human need, and the improvability of human beings and of society itself. The social gospel also sought to replace excessively individualistic conceptions of Christianity with more organic conceptions of the church and of the Kingdom of God in order that these might be a counterbalance to the new concentrations of economic and political power.

Meanwhile, before the end of the nineteenth century, Presbyterians were attempting to reach unchurched urban dwellers by evangelism and by institutional churches and neighborhood houses. In Philadelphia, tent evangelistic services regularly drew hundreds of recently arrived Italians. In Chicago and other cities Presbyterian neighborhood houses and settlement houses provided diversified programs of entertainment, instruction, and worship in the spirit of Christian goodwill. The Board of Home Missions did Christian work in many languages among recent immigrants.

The rush to the cities brought a corresponding depletion of rural areas. As part of his conservation program, President Theodore Roosevelt appointed a Country Life Commission, which reported recommendations in 1908. At about the same time, others made sociological studies of the declining rural church, and in 1910 the Presbyterian Board of Home Missions created a Department of the Church and Country Life. Under the able Warren H. Wilson, this Department, by using the best sociological knowledge and techniques, helped many rural churches to greater Christian effectiveness. Later it was sometimes found effective to combine a number of rural churches to create a "larger parish" under a diversified staff.

Christian Unity. By the late nineteenth century many forces were working to bring the American churches closer together. Some two centuries in the common American environment had developed numerous resemblances and had rubbed off many inherited differences, including many theological differences. The unusually divided state of the

American churches which the home and foreign missionary task confronted cried aloud for closer unity, at a time when interdependence was rapidly increasing in secular life. Since early in the nineteenth century, there had been renewed emphasis on the church. This emphasis now found expression in cooperation and union among churches as churches, and not merely among Christian individuals as in the earlier days of the Benevolent Empire (see Chapter 9).

Presbyterians, in this period between 1861 and 1914, were active in all three kinds of Christian unity—nondenominational cooperation of Christian individuals, church federations, and church mergers. The Presbyterian Church acted with Presbyterian and Reformed Churches of many lands to form in 1875 an important federation, the World Presbyterian Alliance. In 1908 the Presbyterian and about thirty other American churches, with some 17,000,-000 communicant members, organized the Federal Council of the Churches of Christ in America.

Presbyterians were involved in church mergers also. In 1906 the Cumberland Presbyterian Church, which had separated in 1810 (see Chapter 8), reunited with the Presbyterian Church U.S.A., though a minority continued its separate existence. The Cumberland Church's chief strength was in the Border States and in the South, and preparatory to the union the Presbyterian Church amended its Constitution to permit organization of separate black presbyteries and synods. This was barely forty years after Emancipation, but more advanced ideals of racial integration caused the church in 1967 to abolish the provision. This addition of numerous congregations in the South restored to the Presbyterian Church the national character that it had lost at the time of the Civil War. The Presbyterian Church U.S.A. thus became once again a "national" rather than a merely "Northern" church.

Another organic union was with the Welsh Calvinistic Methodist or Presbyterian Church in the United States. In 1828 the first Welsh Calvinistic Methodist presbytery in the United States was organized. In 1870 this church, which was a descendant of the church of the same name in Wales, erected a General Assembly and in 1920 merged with the Presbyterian Church in the U.S.A.

Public Worship. Early English Puritanism, in its controversy with Anglicanism, as we have seen, went far beyond the Reformed Churches of the European continent in seeking for simplicity of worship to emphasize the complete spirituality of God. For the beautiful medieval cathedrals and churches were substituted bare meetinghouses; embellishments of painting and sculpture and stained glass were cast out; elaborate and beautiful ritual was rejected as a spiritual distraction and a snare to the soul. In America this Puritan ideal of simplicity in worship deteriorated under the influence of rude frontier conditions and of emotional revivalism until public worship had become almost slovenly.

Reawakened churchliness in the nineteenth century, however, led some American Presbyterians to new interest in the early Reformed liturgies. A Church Service Society, organized in New York City in the home of Dr. Henry van Dyke in 1897, sought to encourage among Presbyterians worthier ideals of public worship. The new interest bore fruit in 1906 in *The Book of Common Worship,* published under the auspices of the General Assembly for voluntary use in the churches. The book was revised in 1932 and again in 1946 and contained orders of service for public worship, prayers, and forms for many occasions. It was a definite step in the direction of greater dignity and beauty of worship.

13

Wars, Depression, and New Life

Wars and Depression. The most notable world events in the period 1914–1958 were two World Wars and an economic depression that had worldwide impact. The Presbyterian Church was profoundly affected by these upheavals.

The first settlers in Jamestown and especially in New England considered themselves a people chosen by God to fulfill a divine destiny for mankind. This idea became nationalized in the American Revolution and was conspicuous in the expansion across the western frontier. President Woodrow Wilson gave the idea secular expression during World War I in challenging America to "make the world safe for democracy." Many Presbyterian and other ministers preached the war as a great crusade. The Presbyterian General Assembly, in the language of the Confession of Faith, endorsed the war as "just and necessary." Dr. Robert E. Speer, distinguished leader of Presbyterian foreign missions, in supporting the war effort, was among the few who warned against self-righteousness and urged moderation of spirit, for which he was roundly denounced in the public press.

The prevailing naiveté was inevitably followed by deep disillusionment and a national swing to the opposite extreme of widespread pacifism. The Presbyterian General

Assembly, for example, after previously giving hearty and unsuccessful support to the League of Nations, announced in 1934 "its break with the entire war system" and declared that "Christians cannot give their support to war as a method of carrying on international conflict." An effort was made to amend the church's Constitution by emphasizing the individual's conscience and removing the statement that civil government has the right to wage war. But the amendment failed of adoption in 1939. By that time war clouds were again gathering in Europe. Amid these rapid fluctuations, America, including its churchmen, was trying desperately to decide what the nation's role in the world should be.

World War I had stimulated national unity and great financial drives. Learning from this experience, many of the denominations launched money-raising campaigns of their own. Presbyterians had their New Era Movement (1919–1923) for general and financial promotion, but an ambitious interdenominational Interchurch World Movement fell far short of its goals.

For nearly a decade after World War I the nation enjoyed unprecedented economic expansion during which many Presbyterian and other congregations added large church school buildings or erected new Gothic-style cruciform churches with divided chancel, nave, and transept.

A decade of economic depression followed the boom. Church staffs were drastically reduced, debts on new buildings proved unmanageable, and mission budgets often were cut to the bone.

Some historians in retrospect wrote of a "religious depression" in this postwar period and even of a "post-Protestant" era. To be sure, Protestants—among whom Presbyterians constituted a very important element—no longer dominated American culture as they once had. But Protestants, viewed collectively, continued to be by far the largest religious group in the United States, though a minority of the total population.

In World War II the spirit of a holy crusade was quite lacking in the churches. Rather, the struggle was viewed as a grim task that had to be performed. Toward the close of the war the church was active in a World Order Movement, which greatly helped to create in the United States a climate congenial to the founding of the United Nations. Amid the birth pangs of a new era, Presbyterians tried increasingly, though imperfectly, to be guided by Christian norms rather than by any mob passions of the moment. The war was the occasion of important chaplain and relief services, and, following the war, Presbyterians raised a fund of more than $23,000,000 for reconstruction and new Christian work. In the cold war against Communist Russia which followed, the Presbyterian General Assembly's General Council, by "A Letter to Presbyterians" in 1953, spoke vigorously and courageously for freedom and justice against an enslaving fear of Communism that was sweeping the country.

During the closing years of the war and for more than a decade thereafter, there was a noticeable quickening of religious interest in the churches. Church attendance increased noticeably, more religious books were being read, and there was a new seriousness of attitude toward religion. Under the Presbyterian Church's Division of Evangelism, a New Life Movement, cooperating with similar movements in other denominations, reflected and greatly stimulated the new interest. Many persons were brought into the church during these years.

The New Orthodoxy. Starting in the mid-1930's, neo-orthodoxy began to influence Christian thinking in America. In 1919, amid the despair and agony that followed World War I in Europe, Karl Barth declared that the impor-

tant thing for man is to face the basal fact of his existence
—that he is a guilty sinner and must make a right decision
about God. In the spirit of the Protestant Reformation this
neo-orthodoxy insisted that Christian life is personal en-
counter with God and trust in him as revealed in Jesus
Christ. It taught that the Bible is the record of God's revelation of himself, which the Holy Spirit causes to become the
Word of God to the individual believer.

It was in the 1930's, when American self-confidence was
prostrated by the Great Depression, that neo-orthodoxy
entered the Presbyterian and other American churches. It
came just as the rather futile fundamentalist-modernist controversy was waning, and offered a kind of middle ground
on which extremists might unite. It accepted the conclusions of modern critical Biblical scholarship and acknowledged the relativity of culture and of all human values. It
emphasized man's finitude and the reality of human sin, but
insisted that the absolute God, by an inexplicable act of
grace, makes himself known to individual human beings in
a paradoxical "point of contact" by his Spirit. This action
of God's grace is to be received by a "leap of faith." Neo-
orthodoxy was criticized by some for its subtlety and para-
doxes, but it brought a breath of new life to Christian thinking in Europe and America. In Presbyterian classrooms,
pulpits, and pews it contributed to greatly deepened interest in Christian truth. Some, however, lightly bypassing its
profundity and metaphysical subtlety, misconstrued it as an
easy updating of their own traditional theological views.

The Ecumenical Movement. The word "ecumenical" is
from a Greek word meaning "the whole inhabited world,"
or "worldwide." The ecumenical movement is not trying to
organize a superchurch, but to realize spiritual oneness
among Christians throughout the world in fulfillment of

Christ's prayer in John 17:21: "That they may all be one."

The modern ecumenical movement has three principal roots: foreign missions, the application of Christian principles to social problems (called the Life and Work movement), and the search for theological agreement (called the Faith and Order movement).

Foreign missions, before the opening of the twentieth century, had planted the Christian church in every major area of the world. Cooperation among missionary boards and mergers among the younger churches on the field were much in advance of unity movements at home and were pointing the way toward Christian unity on a worldwide basis. The World Missionary Conference at Edinburgh in 1910 was a milestone. Hundreds of scholars from many lands prepared studies for it, and its Continuation Committee paved the way for organizing the International Missionary Council in 1921, which continuously viewed the missionary enterprise in terms of a single global Christian strategy.

The Life and Work movement tried to enlist the wisdom and resources of the churches of the world in order that they might unitedly give Christian guidance to the great social forces, international and domestic, that were remaking modern life. Life and Work took form at a conference in Stockholm, Sweden, in 1925, and was further developed in a conference at Oxford, England, in 1937.

The third root of the ecumenical movement, the Faith and Order movement, heroically addressed itself to a full and frank discussion of the theological issues that keep the churches divided, as well as of the truths that Christians hold in common. Faith and Order held its first conference at Lausanne, Switzerland, in 1927, with a later conference at Edinburgh, Scotland, in 1937. The two movements—Life and Work and Faith and Order—combined to form, at Amsterdam, Holland, in 1948, the World Council of Churches, with more than 150 member churches.

The Presbyterian Church has contributed important leadership and support to all three branches of the ecumenical movement from their beginning. On national and local levels, Presbyterians have shown their ecumenical spirit, among other ways, by helping, in 1950, to combine eight federations to form the National Council of the Churches of Christ in the U.S.A.; by participating actively in numerous state and local federations and cooperative undertakings; and by amending their Constitution frequently to endorse and facilitate Christian unity. As the world is torn by change and animosities, the Christian churches have been increasingly trying to provide spiritual healing and unity.

The Church's World Mission. World War II fanned into a flame the revolt of peoples in Asia and Africa against colonialism. Nations just born struggled heroically against imperialism, poverty, and illiteracy. To anxious millions Russian Communism seemed to promise emancipation and power. In some areas, the reinvigoration of non-Christian religions posed further problems for Christian missions. Meanwhile, as a vigorous new Christianity was arising among non-Christian nations, secularism from within was threatening the so-called Christian nations themselves. Thus by midcentury the whole idea of mission had changed. It was now realized that older and younger churches were partners in a single task—that of bearing witness to the saving power of Jesus Christ against unbelief and paganism in every nation of the world. Mission in this new sense was coming to be recognized as the church's total task at home and abroad.

The Presbyterian Church streamlined its missionary strategy to meet the new situation, especially the rising nationalism. Earlier tendencies to encourage the younger churches to become "self-governing, self-supporting, and self-propagating" were speeded up. Missions were transformed into national churches, with missionaries in such churches taking the new name "fraternal workers," who acted in an advisory capacity while the nationals took over direct leadership. Then, too, national leaders of the so-called younger churches were secured for service on the executive staff of the Presbyterian Board of Foreign Missions.

Even amid world upheaval, the 1,004 Presbyterian missionary and fraternal workers in 1955 could see many signs of promise for the World Church. In spite of terrible war losses, the Korean church had doubled in size within a decade. Brazil had the largest Latin Protestant community in the world. In Mexico, 8 percent of the population had become Protestant. In some Moslem lands the church was making a renewed thrust. Christian work was advancing encouragingly in the Philippines, Thailand, Africa, and in many other fields.

Social Concern. The economic depression of the 1930's, which brought widespread unemployment and suffering, focused attention on serious defects in the American economic system, and caused the General Assembly to take more advanced ground in its economic pronouncements. The Department of Social Education and Action, created by the Board of Christian Education in 1936, gave to the church important leadership in this and other social fields. In 1944, during the economic pressures of World War II, the Assembly voiced large Christian views on industrial relations, confessing the church's economic and social sins, and asserting the obligation of Christians to foster in economic pressure groups—such as industry, labor, agriculture, consumers—a desire to serve the welfare of all.

Vast population movements within the country, which increased by the migration of workers to defense plants during World War II and continued after the war, created problems for the church. The migration of blacks from the rural South to cities in the North greatly accelerated. Cities continued to expand, not only in the Northeastern and North Central States but on the Pacific Coast and in the South. Large housing projects became a new mission field. The problem of the decay and renewal of downtown areas, the inner city, was particularly acute, and in 1954 the Board of National Missions appointed a Special Committee on the Inner City. As the movement away from farms continued, Presbyterians made increasing use of the Larger Parish Plan, in which nearby rural congregations combined forces to secure a staff of ministers performing specialized functions. Among the promising areas of America to enjoy development in this era was Alaska, where the Board of National Missions was aiding some thirty churches.

The churches, like American secular institutions, had been deeply involved in racial segregation. But by the 1950's the situation was giving them pangs of conscience and there were signs of promise. In 1954 the General Assembly appointed a Special Committee to confer with the synods and presbyteries of the church that were organized on the basis of race or language, and two years later the Assembly approved the merger of the Synod of Oklahoma and the former black Synod of Canadian. A few congregations were becoming integrated and a very few were being served by an interracial ministry. At least a beginning was being made in "operation desegregation."

Women's Work. One of the important developments since the Presbyterian reunion of 1869 has been the increasingly prominent position officially accorded to women in the work of the Presbyterian Church. In 1870 the Woman's Foreign Missionary Society was organized in the church, followed in 1879 by the organization of the Woman's Board of Home Missions. In 1915 an amendment to the Constitution authorized the election of deaconesses. In 1923 women were made eligible to membership on all the denominational Boards and to membership on the General Council, while a Constitutional amendment in 1930 opened to them the office of ruling elder. The office of commissioned church worker, recognized by the church's Constitution in 1948, was from the beginning open to women, and finally in 1956 women were made eligible to the ordained ministry.

The Church and Education. A notable achievement of the Presbyterian Church was the launching of its new *Christian Faith and Life* curriculum for church schools in October, 1948. Utilizing the cooperation of parents for homework, it issued attractively illustrated and designed materials, many of them as bound books. In recurring three-year cycles it dealt with the themes Christ, the Bible, the Christian church. Based on fresh and contemporary theological thinking, it was a kind of pioneering effort among the denomination's official documents in creative theological restatement. Possessing ecumenical outlook and missionary interest, the curriculum emphasized personal commitment to Christ. If it had a flaw, it was perhaps the level of demand it made on parents and volunteer teachers.

A notable addition to religious journalism in America was *Presbyterian Life*. When it was started in 1949 the magazine had a circulation of 80,982; by the summer of 1957 it had a list of regular subscribers that passed the million mark. Written in an ecumenical spirit, avoiding a too-narrow denominationalism, and with its interesting pictures, attractive format, and popularly written articles, it helped to keep Presbyterians everywhere informed on the work of the Kingdom.

Presbyterian church school enrollment reflected the widely discussed religious awakening of these years, increasing by more than one third in the decade following World War II—nearly three times as much as the rate of population increase. The church expanded its lay leadership training programs and increased the number of directors of Christian education in the local churches to nearly 800. Summer conferences and camps expanded to reach more than 45,000 young people in 1956, giving instruction and recreation, and inspiring many to choose Christian service vocations.

The characteristic interest of Presbyterians in education increased during these years. In 1956 forty-one colleges were affiliated with the Presbyterian Church, with an enrollment of nearly 30,000 students and an investment of more than $143,000,000. The Board of Christian Education represented the church in relations with the colleges, and a Presbyterian College Union also fostered their common interests. In addition, Presbyterian Westminster Foundations were conducting Christian work on 144 non-Presbyterian campuses, ministering to as many as possible of the estimated quarter million Presbyterian youth in the secular colleges and universities of the land.

The church's program of adult work—much of it administrative and functional rather than educational in character—developed greatly. A National Council of Women's Organizations met every four years, later every three, to give guidance to women's work in the local churches, presbyteries, and synods. Men of the church organized a National Council of Presbyterian Men in 1948, which grew from 177 chapters at the end of the first year to 2,516 chapters seven years later. The Council, which was composed of lay representatives from the church's presbyteries, boards, and agencies, and of ministerial representatives from the synods, sought to encourage Presbyterian men to organize for the work of the church on the local, presbyterial, and national levels.

The church showed increasing interest in educating its candidates for the ministry. Starting in 1941, the theological seminaries received a percentage of the church's total benevolence giving. A Council of Theological Education was organized in 1943 under the authority of the General Assembly, with representatives from all of the seminaries and Boards, and also representatives from the church at large. Its purpose was to call the attention of the church to the needs of the seminaries, to help the seminaries to cooperate with one another, and to relate their work as closely as possible to the church. Reflecting perhaps a general quickening of religious interest in the church and nation, the seminaries as a whole experienced a substantial increase in enrollment. Changing times brought changes in curriculum with further changes in prospect, such as supervision of fieldwork and new interest in pastoral counseling.

14

The United
Presbyterian Church
of North America

Ancestors of the United Presbyterian Church of
North America. In 1958 the Presbyterian Church in the
United States of America and the United Presbyterian
Church of North America merged to form The United Pres-
byterian Church in the United States of America. Chapters
6 to 10 and 12 and 13 have dealt with the history of the
Presbyterian Church in the U.S.A. The present chapter will
sketch the history of the United Presbyterian Church of
North America to 1958 and Chapter 14 will then discuss the
history since 1958 of the church created by this union.

The United Presbyterian Church of North America has
been the principal representative in our country of the Scottish "dissenting" churches, that is, the Covenanters and the
Seceders (see Chapter 4). This has been a difficult as well
as an important role. The Scottish Covenants and other
special issues that gave birth to these churches were rooted
in Scottish history and could not easily be transplanted to
America. The struggles in Scotland had stimulated strong
convictions and independence of spirit. These qualities, in
spite of the fact that the groups in America were of the same
nationality and very similar in beliefs, for a long time made
unity among them very difficult. The story of the United
Presbyterian Church of North America is in brief the story
of successfully uniting and preserving this heroic heritage

and of relating it to contemporary American life.

Scattered Covenanters and Seceders from both Scotland and northern Ireland settled in New York, southeastern Pennsylvania, and South Carolina, and later moved west. Western Pennsylvania eventually became their chief stronghold. In a colorful ceremony at Middle Octorara, Pennsylvania, in 1743, Covenanters "renewed the Covenants" with drawn swords, reminding them of the perils faced by their ancestors in the days of Charles II and James II. John Cuthbertson, first Covenanter minister to settle in the colonies, came in 1751. He traveled on horseback some 70,000 miles through forests and across rivers, in danger of Indians and wild animals, sometimes sleeping outdoors in rain or snow, preaching, counseling, administering the sacraments, exercising church discipline. "Tired but safe," he wrote in his diary at the end of a busy day. In 1774, with two other Covenanter ministers, Cuthbertson organized the Reformed Presbytery of America. In 1753, the Seceders, the other principal root of the United Presbyterian Church of North America, organized under the name Associate Presbytery of Pennsylvania.

In the Revolutionary War, Covenanters and Seceders ardently supported the patriot side. If they could unite in supporting American independence, why not unite in one church, which would be independent of the church bodies and historic controversies of the mother country? This was done, and in 1782 Covenanters and Seceders united to form the Associate Reformed Church.

The union was a statesmanlike one, but it faced many difficulties. Some Covenanters and some Seceders declined to enter the union and continued their independent bodies. In the 1820's, for geographical as well as ecclesiastical reasons, the Associate Reformed Church itself divided into a number of independent bodies. Its Synod of Carolina organized what has since become the General Synod of the Associate Reformed Presbyterian Church, located in the South. Another portion united with the Presbyterian Church in the U.S.A. But the larger part of the church reunited in 1856 to constitute the General Synod of the Associate Reformed Church.

The Formation of the United Presbyterian Church of North America. A new day dawned for the family of Scottish dissenting churches with the formation of the United Presbyterian Church of North America in 1858. Differences over methods of defining the distinctive beliefs that these churches held in common almost wrecked union hopes. But laymen were eager for closer cooperation, and union triumphed. On May 26, 1858, delegates of the General Synod of the Associate Reformed Church met delegates from the Synod of the Associate Presbyterian Church (Seceders) at Seventh and Smithfield Streets in what is now Pittsburgh's "golden triangle" and marched together to the old City Hall to celebrate the union of these two churches to form the United Presbyterian Church of North America. Reformed Presbyterians (Covenanters) who had declined to accompany other Covenanters into the earlier union of 1782 had negotiated for a time, but once again remained separate. Thus, at the time of this union in 1958, except for the Associate Reformed Presbyterian Church, with a membership of 27,467 located in the South and the Reformed Presbyterian Church in North America (General Synod), with 1,279 members, and the Reformed Presbyterian Church of North America (Old School), with 6,382 members, and the Associate Presbyterian Church of North America, with 470, the United Presbyterian Church of North America, with its membership of 251,344, included all the direct ecclesiastical heirs in America of Covenanters and Seceders.

Those who were about to unite in 1858 held two conventions in the months before the union. Covenanters and Seceders were strict in their orthodoxy and had a deep devotional quality in their personal faith, but had never been identified with American revivalism. A religious revival in 1857–1858, however, was at the moment filling many of their congregations, and was conspicuous in these conventions. Many in convention confessed the churches' sins, including the sin of disunity, and in prolonged discussions inquired how the churches, by Biblical rather than by sensational methods, might receive God's fullest blessing. These earnest meetings did much to set the tone of the union of 1858 and of the United Presbyterian Church of North America, which was there formed.

The basis for the union of 1858 was the Westminster Confession of Faith, the Larger and Shorter Catechisms, and a "Judicial Testimony" consisting of eighteen declarations, the last five of which set forth the new church's "distinctives," that is, the particular views that distinguished it (and its predecessors) from other churches. The five "distinctives" were: (1) opposition to slavery; (2) refusal to admit to communicant membership members of oathbound secret societies; (3) invitation to the Lord's Supper restricted to those who adhere to the church's distinctive tenets; (4) endorsement of the principle of covenanting; and (5) the exclusive use of the psalms for singing in worship. The slavery issue ended with the Civil War, and the other four "distinctives" were officially abandoned in 1925.

Developments Since 1858. Hardly was the United Presbyterian Church of North America created in 1858 before the Civil War was upon the country. With the distinguished antislavery record of its parent churches, the new church in 1863 undertook work among some 10,000 black refugees who had sought freedom behind Federal army lines in Nashville, Tennessee. Like all refugees, they lacked homes, clothing, food. Within a month, the United Presbyterian missionary, Rev. Joseph G. McKee, was ministering to the sick, supplying the necessities of life, and had opened a school to which old and young flocked. In 1875, Knoxville College was founded for "Freedmen" in Knoxville, Tennessee. The church's work for blacks later expanded to include churches and schools in Kentucky, Tennessee, Virginia, North Carolina, and Alabama.

The women of the church have done notable work, starting a Women's General Missionary Society in 1883 which was active in nearly every area of the church's home and foreign missions. In 1888 this Society created an Annual Thank-offering, which over the years raised hundreds of thousands of dollars. After the rise of Christian Endeavor and of local young people's societies, the church in 1889 held the first national convention of its Young People's Christian Union. In more recent years the program was reconstructed along age group lines. The church had two colleges in Egypt and one in Pakistan, in addition to six in the United States: Muskingum in Ohio (founded in 1837), Westminster in Pennsylvania (1852), Monmouth in Illinois (1853), Knoxville in Tennessee (1875), Tarkio in Missouri (1883), and Sterling in Kansas (1887). The church also had three theological seminaries: Pittsburgh-Xenia in Pittsburgh, which had early roots in both of the parent churches, and seminaries in Cairo, Egypt, and Gujranwala, Pakistan. Pittsburgh-Xenia Seminary later united with Western Theological Seminary to form Pittsburgh Theological Seminary.

By a series of Board consolidations starting in 1923, the church reduced its Boards to five: Administration (for coordinating and promoting the general work of the church), American Missions (formerly Home Missions), Foreign Missions, Christian Education, and Ministerial Pensions and Relief. The Board of American Missions and its predecessors, in addition to aiding young and needy churches, through the years developed such diversified service as work among Mormons, Sunday School missions, work among mountaineers and among immigrants, evangelism, social service, church erection.

In 1854 the Associate Presbyterian Synod had elected Andrew Gordon to be its pioneer missionary to India. Others had declined appointment, but Gordon and his young wife accepted it heartily as a being a call from God. Sailing on a freighter on which they had to build their own bunks, they reached India early in 1855. It took two years to win three converts. But the work grew and prospered. In 1854 the Associate Reformed Church had started missionary work in Egypt. The United Presbyterian Church inherited and enlarged these beginnings until work was carried on in five lands abroad: India, Pakistan, Egypt, The Sudan (begun in 1900), and Abyssinia (1919). The home church maintained unusually close relations with the foreign field and was consistently among the highest of American churches in per capita gifts to missions. Nearly a quarter of the church's membership was in Asia and Africa, and its second largest synod was in Pakistan.

The first General Assembly after World War I, in 1919, voted unanimously to prepare a revised Statement of Faith as a part of the "reconstruction duty" of "the new era." It was felt that the Westminster Confession was "falling into disuse" and did not in every detail represent the church's contemporary beliefs, so that subscription to it was "commonly accompanied with reservations." A Confessional Statement, which summarized in clear modern language and which slightly modified the teaching of the Westminster Confession, was adopted in 1925. The Preamble to it says, "This Statement . . . takes the place of the Testimony of 1858, and wherever it deviates from the Westminster Standards its declarations are to prevail."

The Statement was an important milestone in the church's history. By replacing the Judicial Testimony of 1858 it officially discarded the church's "distinctives," and opened the way for closer fellowship and unity with other Christian churches. This Statement showed, too, that the church's venerable heritage of Covenants and later of written Testimonies, while originally having the effect of making the Confession tighter and stricter, could be used in the opposite direction of a vigorous progressivism. The inherited ideal of the church's living voice was finding new expression.

The ideal of Christian unity played a conspicuous and growing role in the history of the United Presbyterians. In the century before 1858, their parent churches struggled unsuccessfully for durable unity among themselves in the face of detailed, conscientious differences. The union of 1858, which created the United Presbyterian Church of North America, was a major turning point. During three quarters of the years from 1858 until 1957 this church was actively negotiating some church union. In the nineteenth century, conversations were usually with smaller Presbyterian and Reformed bodies, whereas in the twentieth century extended negotiations were conducted with larger bodies also, some of the proposals being to unite simultaneously with more than one church.

In 1910, as one of the earlier church bodies to take such action, the General Assembly set up a Permanent Committee on Church Relations to guide the church in cooperation and union. The United Presbyterians were members of the World Presbyterian Alliance, the National Council of Churches, and the World Council of Churches. The church's history is a dynamic one. It is the story of a body of Christians with strong and precisely defined convictions who periodically, after searching discussion, related anew their heritage to changing American conditions.

The United Presbyterian Church in the U.S.A. An important union of American Presbyterian bodies occurred in 1958 when the Presbyterian Church in the U.S.A. and the United Presbyterian Church of North America voted to merge under the name "The United Presbyterian Church in the U.S.A." This merger was consummated in Pittsburgh on May 28, 1958. There had been intermittent talk of such a union since soon after the Civil War, a concerted mutual effort toward it in 1934, and continuous official negotiations since 1951, when a three-way union including also the Southern Presbyterians was being considered. When that three-way union did not materialize, the two General Assemblies in 1955 authorized the drafting of a Plan of Union to unite the two churches, and the next year submitted the finished Plan to their respective presbyteries. The presbyteries approved, and the two Assemblies gave final confirmation in 1957. As in Scotland in 1929, heirs of Scottish establishment and dissent were at last reunited.

The Constitution of the church created by this union of 1958 consisted of three doctrinal standards: The Westminster Confession of Faith and the Larger and Shorter Catechisms; and of three governmental standards: the Directory for the Worship of God, the Form of Government, and the Book of Discipline—all six embodying the historic faith and practice of the two churches. A Special Committee on Consolidations was set up to recommend in due time appropriate consolidation of synods and presbyteries and of boards, agencies, and other institutions of the two churches.

The presbyteries and General Assembly of the Presbyterian Church in the U.S.A. favored union almost unanimously. The General Assembly of the United Presbyterian Church, after a divided vote on union, unanimously adopted the following resolution: "It is resolved by the Ninety-ninth General Assembly that we enter into the union of our church and the Presbyterian Church U.S.A. with faith, hope, and love and the prayerful purpose of making the union a happy and effective means of advancing the Kingdom of Jesus Christ, our Savior and Lord." In this spirit the united church looked forward to a larger and greater future under the guidance of God.

15

Since
the 1950's

Social Concerns. The postwar quickening of religious interest faded by the end of the 1950's and was followed in the 1960's by a period of upheavals, deep self-searching, and creative change both in the American nation and in the churches. Most conspicuous among the forces producing this change were the "black revolt" and the Vietnam war.

The black revolt gained momentum on a bus in Montgomery, Alabama, when a tired black woman refused to yield her seat to a white in accordance with a local ordinance. Dr. Martin Luther King, Jr., who had studied principles of nonviolent resistance taught by Henry D. Thoreau and Mohandas Gandhi, came to the fore as the leader of a powerful movement of protest. The movement steadily accelerated and in 1963, Dr. King, in a memorable oration, told a crowd of some 250,000 black and white freedom marchers in Washington, D.C., "I Have a Dream." Under mounting public pressures President Lyndon Johnson and Congress abolished statutory segregation. But when Dr. King turned north and led marches protesting conditions in Northern ghettos, he testified that he had never, in all of the South, faced such bitterness. Adopting a very different approach, other black leaders in 1966 proclaimed the ideal of "black power," a phrase which could be variously interpreted.

The Presbyterian Church had previously made pronouncements supporting civil rights, but in 1963, while tension in the nation was mounting rapidly, the General Assembly took creative action. It set up a Commission on Religion and Race with its own executive director and staff and with a budget of $600,000 for its first three years. The most notable achievement of this commission was the self-examination with which it confronted the church. In ensuing years the Assembly, on recommendation of this Commission, instructed its boards, judicatories, and congregations to see that their electing and hiring processes were free of racial bias. The church in previous pronouncements had counseled society on these matters but now it attempted the much more difficult and important systematic examination of its own practice. Within less than a decade and a half the church had elected three black Moderators of the General Assembly and a number of other blacks to positions of high responsibility. These actions spoke more loudly than did a whole generation of pronouncements.

But only a beginning had been made. As statutory segregation ended in the South, the Commission directed attention to the more persistent problems of the Northern ghettos—housing, schooling, employment. By 1967 the Commission was lamenting that interest in racial justice was already declining and that "the gap between the Negro poor and the rest of our society has probably widened during the life of the Commission." The Commission approved and commended to the attention of the church the National Committee of Negro Churchmen's endorsement of the concept of black power.

In the 1970's the Council on Church and Race (its name

had been changed in 1968) was stressing the theology of liberation which had strong exponents in Latin America as well as in the United States. Many minority groups in addition to the blacks were now attaining a new self-awareness and were demanding greater autonomy. The church was becoming ethnically more pluralistic as a conscious expression of the two separate but related ideals of Christian freedom and cultural freedom.

This period also saw the ending of racially segregated judicatories. In 1967 a committee that had conducted negotiations on this problem was able to announce to the General Assembly that the last of the racially segregated presbyteries had united with the white judicatory of the area.

Contemporaneous with the black revolt as a cause of upheaval and change in the 1960's was the Vietnam war. Evening newscasts brought battle scenes into the living room, vividly portraying the wounded and the dying. Then there was the daily "body count" of enemies slain, reported like basketball scores. Was this the American Dream or a ghastly nightmare?

Amid increasing tension the Presbyterian Church attempted the difficult task of speaking in a way that was both distinctively Christian and humanly practicable. In 1960 the General Assembly warned of "a growing confusion between the beliefs we still profess as a people and the values we actually live by." Three years later the Assembly suggested that American Christians introduce into policy on Vietnam some of the broader ecumenical perspectives being currently offered on the war by Asian Christians and by the World Council of Churches. By 1966 the Assembly noted the widespread dissent among university faculties and students and the search by students for standards by which to live. This Assembly struck a timely Christian note in declaring that "no nation is righteous before God; therefore we ought not to suppose our cause completely just or our motives completely pure." Amid the futile brutalities of the Vietnam war, Americans were becoming aware of the dangerous self-righteousness which from the beginning had lurked in the American tradition of a divine national destiny. The answer, the Assembly of 1968 advised, is not for the United States to "recoil in disillusionment from its international responsibilities."

The invasion of Cambodia created an explosion on college and seminary campuses. The Assembly of 1970 angrily declared: "Without the consent or knowledge of our Congress, to promote the success of a war in which our very participation has been grievously questioned by the American people, we have invaded a sovereign and legally neutral nation. . . . We have called into question our national integrity both at home and abroad." After the President had defended continuance of the war in order to win a peace with honor, the General Assembly of 1972 declared: "There is no honor for America in continued deception about the origins and intent of the policy pursued by our government since 1954. . . . We have subjected Vietnam to a terror seldom before known in warfare." When the nation finally withdrew from the war with none of its objectives accomplished, disillusionment was deep and bitter. After the Watergate burglary and cover-up resulted in the early 1970's in the resignation of a President of the United States who had posed as champion of law and order, distrust of government—and, to a degree, of every centralized institution—was further increased. The Presbyterian and other churches were being confronted with the task of supplying relevant spiritual and moral guidance for a distraught society.

One of the most prominent social concerns both of the

church and of the nation during this period was the rights and opportunities of women. As previously noted, women had been admitted to the ordained ministry in 1956, but churches—sometimes including especially women church members—were often reluctant to call them as senior pastors. Even in nonpastoral church vocations their recognition and rank were often below what merit warranted. Task forces and pronouncements at every judicatorial level pressed their claims on the church and on society at large. In 1971 the General Assembly elected its first woman Moderator.

In this period the church developed further its practice which had been growing since the early nineteenth century of seeking to stimulate the thinking of Christians about their social obligations. The General Assembly repeatedly declared that its social pronouncements did not have the force of church law but were intended to stimulate Christian thinking and Christian social response. The Advisory Council on Church and Society, as it came to be called, researched individual social problems in depth, enlisting the services not only of theologians and pastors but also of professional specialists in the field being explored. Such issues as church and state, international relations, hunger, poverty, housing, family life, homosexuality, old age, penology, alcohol, labor, church investments were among the numerous topics individually treated in depth. There were those who felt that such matters were not a proper concern of the church which, they felt, should devote itself to winning individuals to Christian faith; others considered social concern a central obligation of the gospel. This tended toward an unnatural cleavage between "private Christians" and "public Christians," but most Presbyterians considered the connection between Christian roots and fruits to be inseparable.

The Confession of 1967. The committee that drafted the Confession of 1967 was laboring during the peak of the turbulent sixties and was keenly aware of the moral significance of the social changes that were taking place. The committee was created in 1958 by the first General Assembly of the newly organized United Presbyterian Church in the U.S.A., and presented its completed draft to the Assembly of 1965. When the document was transmitted to the presbyteries to secure the constitutionally needed acceptance by two thirds of the presbyteries, it won a sweeping endorsement, as it did also from the Assemblies of 1966 and 1967. Of the church's 188 presbyteries, endorsement by 125 was needed, but 166 approved it, with only 19 presbyteries voting in the negative and 3 not replying. Thus more than 88 percent of all the presbyteries approved the new Confession. This was a notable and encouraging accomplishment, especially when compared with the inability of the church in the early 1890's to achieve any updating of its doctrinal standards and the very limited revision which was finally attained in 1903. Definite theological guidance was now available for presbyteries as they ordained ministerial candidates, for denominational agencies in the preparation of church literature and other forms of assistance, for worship, and for mission of every kind.

The new Confession is clearly Christocentric and Trinitarian, though the non-Biblical term "Trinity" is not used. The Confession centers in the idea of "reconciliation," which conveniently provides both a "vertical" (God to man) and a "horizontal" (man to man) axis, laying the foundation for strong ethical emphasis so greatly needed by the times. Following the guidance of Biblical theology and Biblical patterns, the Confession bypasses metaphysics and portrays God as the One who has acted and ever continues to act in redemptive love. Accordingly, traditional natural theology is omitted as a major evidence of God, though it is stated that "the world reflects to the eye of faith the majesty and mystery of its Creator."

While the metaphysics of Christ's two natures and one person of the ancient creeds is avoided, "our Lord Jesus Christ" is declared to be "the eternal Son of the Father, who became man." Like the traditional creeds, the Confession discusses Father, Son, and Holy Spirit, but, following the order of the Apostolic Benediction, treats the Son first as the one who by reconciliation makes the Father known. Throughout runs the breadth of God's love and outreach. "The risen Christ is the savior for all men." Human sin is exposed in its range and subtlety: "All human virtue, when seen in the light of God's love in Jesus Christ, is found to be infected by self-interest and hostility." The note of hope is sounded: "The resurrection of Jesus is God's sign that he will consummate his work of creation and reconciliation beyond death and bring to fulfillment the new life begun in Christ." God's revelation is Jesus Christ himself, "the Word of God incarnate," attested by the Holy Spirit through the Bible, the historical conditioning of which is clearly stated.

Perhaps the most original aspects of this fresh statement of the faith are its extended treatment of ethics which is consistently based on the gospel of God's reconciling work rather than on philosophy or intuition, with Jesus Christ himself as the supreme pattern. The church, which "gathers to praise God" and "disperses to serve God," properly exists in "a wide variety of forms." As distinct from God's self-revelation, "the Christian religion," like the Bible, is conditioned by history. By contrast, there runs throughout the Confession the implication that God himself, by an unfathomable mystery, transcends history, in addition to being immanent in history. As examples of where the church's reconciling influence is needed, the Confession describes contemporary problems of race, war, poverty, and sex. In the breadth and extent of its involvement in society, the Confession is much closer to the Reformed faith of the Reformation era than is criticism of this stance. In discussing "The Equipment of the Church," it places preaching in the context of prayer (whose five traditional parts are distinguished) and of the sacraments, which are both interpreted in terms of reconciliation. The Confession nobly declares: "God's redeeming work in Jesus Christ embraces the whole of man's life: social and cultural, economic and political, scientific and technological, individual and corporate." This sentence summarizes one of the broadest and finest aspects of historic Calvinism. The Confession closes with a Biblical ascription of praise to God.

Before the committee drafted the Confession of 1967 it proposed to the church a "Book of Confessions" consisting of eight creedal statements with the new confession to be the ninth. The committee added three confessions of the Reformation era—the Scots Confession, the Heidelberg Catechism, and the Second Helvetic Confession—to the Westminster Confession of Faith and Shorter Catechism, while omitting the very wordy Larger Catechism from the church's existing doctrinal standards. Adding these three sixteenth-century Scottish and Continental confessions to the seventeenth-century more scholastic Westminster documents presented the Reformed faith with greater historical perspective and breadth. It also related the church more closely to its sister Reformed churches of Continental origin. The committee prefixed these Reformation-era documents with the Nicene Creed and the Apostles' Creed, reminding the church of its ecumenical character and the basic heritage that it shared with all Christian churches. As an admirable example of a recent confession the committee included the Theological Declaration of Barmen, a product of the heroic Confessing Church of Germany in the face of Hitler's tyranny. These eight, together with the new Confession of 1967, were approved by the United Presbyterian Church in 1967 as its doctrinal standard under the title *The Book of Confessions.*

The other very important proposal of this committee was also adopted by the church, the alteration of the so-called subscription formula. Two changes were particularly significant. Previously ministers and others were asked at ordination, "Do you believe the Scriptures of the Old and New Testaments to be the Word of God, the only infallible rule of faith and practice?" This was amended to read, "Do you accept the Scriptures of the Old and New Testaments to be the unique and authoritative witness to Jesus Christ in the Church catholic, and by the Holy Spirit God's Word to you?" Nothing was now said about infallibility. The other important change involved the former question, "Do you sincerely receive and adopt the Confession of Faith and the Catechisms of this Church, as containing the system of doctrine taught in the Holy Scriptures?" For more than a century there had been debate as to the meaning of adopting the "system of doctrine," and more recently Biblical theology had questioned whether the Bible taught a "system" of theology as such. This question was therefore changed to read, "Will you perform the duties of a minister of the gospel [these four words being appropriately changed for other offices] in obedience to Jesus Christ, under the authority of the Scriptures and under the continuing guidance of the confessions of this Church?" It will be noticed that this is no longer merely an intellectual affirmation but a course of action rooted in the "authority" of the Scriptures and the "guidance" of the confessions.

For many decades the church had attempted a holding operation in theology, surrendering outposts where necessity seemed to dictate but not attempting a fresh address to the drastically changed cultural situation. Now the church had an entirely fresh statement constructed to speak directly to the times both in theology and ethics. The church immediately put the new Confession to use in worship and in defining Christian social duty.

Ministry, Laity, and the Church. The great expansion in the variety of religious activities in the early nineteenth century produced diversified types of ministry. Previously the concern of presbyteries had been limited mostly to examining and ordaining candidates for pastoral service, overseeing pastors and their churches, and dealing with cases of discipline. But with the diversification of religious activity, ministers became editors of church papers, home and foreign missionaries, secretaries of voluntary societies, administrators of other religious enterprises, chaplains, seminary professors, etc. Later still, ministries became diversified even within the parish itself.

It was not until the twentieth century, and particularly under the stimulus of the ecumenical discussions, that Americans gave extended theological thought to what they had long been treating merely as procedural matters. Questions arose as to where the church itself began and ended. Was the church confined to the parish and to the ascending judicatories above the parish, or did the church in some sense include what the diversified ministries outside the parish were doing? In the increasingly mobile society, less time was spent in the family context. The family parish was still supremely important for dealing with people in a family and residential context, but how were people to be reached while at work or recreation, detached individuals, people continually in transit, and many other special types of whom there were an increasing number? And what was the rela-

tionship, if any, between a minister's nonecclesiastical em-
ployer and the presbytery's constitutional jurisdiction over
the minister's person?

Christians of different heritages in the ecumenical movement, confronting varied practices of church and ministry,
were devoting fresh thought to these problems. Meanwhile
Biblical theology was pointing out that the distinction between "clergy" and "laity" was not a New Testament idea.
This discovery was in accord with the mainline Protestant
Reformers' doctrine of the universal priesthood of believers
(which, however, they did not fully implement) and was
quite congenial to long-developing American traditions of
lay activity and influence. On the practical level some presbyteries found their ministerial rolls filled with nonparish
clergy outvoting the ruling elders who were elected on the
basis of one ruling elder representative for every parish
minister. This particular problem was readily solved by
granting to church sessions additional representatives in
presbytery in proportion to their congregational membership.

But the larger problems still remained. Should there be
different types of requirement for ordination to the different types of ministry? And what would this do to the long-
standing Presbyterian concept of "the parity of the clergy"?
The high mobility of the ministry, not only between
parishes but also from one type of ministry to another,
meant that if there was to be only one type of ordination,
it must include qualification for pastoral service which was
still by far the largest single area of ministerial activity.
Elective courses, which seminaries had developed extensively in the twentieth century, gave some opportunity for
preparation for special ministries even while providing the
basic training for pastoral service.

Between 1958 and 1972 two able special General Assem-

bly committees on the ministry served in succession. Under
the auspices of the first committee a special study, *The
Church and Its Changing Ministry,* was published. Seminars
were held throughout the church, attended by more than
5,000 ministers and 4,000 lay people. This committee
finally reported that after careful survey it found as yet
insufficient consensus to warrant constitutional amendments. The second committee's proposed amendments
were defeated by the presbyteries by a slight majority. Later
replies from the presbyteries revealed that they had not
liked the proposal to give to sessions the right to empower
lay people to administer the sacraments locally or the proposal to change the title "minister" to "continuing member
of presbytery." But the presbyteries had viewed favorably
the committee's effort to establish criteria for membership
in presbytery and also the committee's concept that the
ministry of the church is one. Clearly the church was seeking to achieve a more vital concept of lay ministry.

Meanwhile a special General Assembly Committee on
the Laity saw some polarity between clergy and laity partly
related to differences on social questions. The committee
therefore proposed greater emphasis on the ministry of the
laity, with the added suggestion that elders be more frequently chosen not only on the basis of their service to the
local congregation but also on the basis of their prophetic
Christian ministry to the larger society outside the church.

This still left the presbyteries without clear guidance as
to the kinds of nonparish service for which they might appropriately ordain candidates and on the even more sensi-
tive question as to the circumstances under which they
should erase from the ministerial rolls a minister who had
entered what was on the borderline of nonministerial employment. Some presbyteries tended to construe the matter
strictly, confining ordination to types of work that could not

properly be performed without ordination; other presbyteries construed matters more broadly, granting ordination where it seemed evident that ordination might make the work spiritually more effective. Further thought and wider consensus on this and related matters were needed.

An increasingly acute problem in the late twentieth century was mobility within the pastoral ministry, which had been accelerating ever since the eighteenth century. From the beginning of American Presbyterianism no ecclesiastical power could impose a pastor on an unwilling congregation. But a presbytery, after careful deliberation, did have the power to remove a pastor. Ministerial relations committees, created in the twentieth century, rendered valuable service in preventing unpromising pastorates from being formed, and in counseling cases where friction had developed; but the only contribution they could make to the problem of relocating a displaced minister was to use their good offices of recommendation. The General Assembly on its part maintained an agency to receive information from ministers and from other professional church workers as well as from churches and other employing organizations seeking such persons. This proved helpful, but of course lacked any power to "place" dislocated ministers. The basic problem of displaced ministers still remained, leaving some ministers disillusioned and with wasted talents and training.

New Guides for Worship. In 1955 the General Assembly created a new Special Committee on the Book of Common Worship, which was joined two years later by a similar committee from the (Southern) Presbyterian Church in the United States so that the final results were joint products of the cooperating churches. A quite different book, the Directory for the Worship of God, was the church's constitutional document for the guidance of public worship which theoretically underlay the existing *Book of Common Worship*. But the Directory had been adopted in 1788 as a revision of the Directory drafted by the seventeenth-century Westminster Assembly and ten of its sixteen chapters had received no alteration whatever since 1788. When the Westminster Directory and the Directory of 1788 were drafted, it was without any anticipation that they would be supplemented by worship books. They therefore concentrated principally on describing how the various services were to be conducted, and offered very little material on the theological ideas underlying worship. This was a serious deficiency in the late twentieth century, for by that time theological thought on the nature of the church, the ministry, the sacraments, and the liturgy had been greatly enriched from within the Reformed and Presbyterian Churches and also by contributions from other Protestant churches and notably from creative Roman Catholic thinking. The Special Committee therefore asked and received from the Assembly permission to propose revision of the Directory for Worship itself before proceeding to their original assignment to revise *The Book of Common Worship*.

In 1960 the committee presented to the General Assembly a completely new Directory for Worship, which during the next year was approved by an overwhelming majority of the presbyteries and thus became one of the three normative documents in the church's *Book of Order*.

The new Directory revived some ideas of John Calvin—such as the idea that the Lord's Supper is normative of public worship and that its weekly celebration should be encouraged. The new book throughout was informed by the creative liturgical thinking that had been enriching theological dialogue across denominational lines since the late nineteenth century. The Directory struck a solid Reformed note in declaring: "In worship the initiative belongs with

God" who "redeems men into communion with himself."
"In public worship Jesus Christ in Scripture, sermon, and
sacrament confronts men," though God speaks to people
elsewhere also. The new Directory challenged the excessive
subjectivism and introspection of the American revivalistic
tradition when it declared: "Hymns and other music should
center not upon the worshiper but upon him who is worshiped." Worship should be characterized by both liberty
and orderliness. Emphasis is laid on fellowship in the
church which is the "community of faith." "All believers
participate . . . in the ministry" and therefore the congregation should participate as extensively as possible in the worship—in corporate confession, and in other prayers, and in
responding "Amen" to prayers led by the minister, in
creedal affirmation, in receiving the sacraments, in the offering, in congregational singing, and in the singing of the
choir which "should be drawn as far as practicable from the
congregation itself."

Baptism and the Lord's Supper, as sacraments of the
corporate church, should ordinarily be administered at a
church service where Scripture is expounded. In Baptism
the congregation should be asked to share responsibility for
the child's spiritual growth. In the Lord's Supper, God
offers "continued spiritual nourishment." It is Christ's
Table and "he invites those who put their trust in him to
share in the feast." Nothing is said about formal membership in any church as a condition of admission to the Supper. "The breaking of the bread and the pouring of the wine
show forth that Christ gave his own body to be broken and
his life to be poured out on man's behalf." The Supper
should be the culmination of worship and not be isolated
from other parts of the service. The earlier Presbyterian use
of the Supper as an instrument of church discipline fostered
an utterly unevangelical concept that one must be "worthy"

in order to partake of it. This the new Directory admirably corrected by declaring that "participation in the sacrament is to be understood as a privilege given to the undeserving, rather than a right conferred upon the worthy."

The chapter on marriage enjoins upon the minister previous instruction of the couple. "If the minister is convinced that Christian commitment and responsibility are lacking, and that the marriage is not one which offers promise of being blessed by God, he shall not perform the ceremony." "Such music as accompanies the ceremony should direct attention to God." "Excessive expense and ostentation should be avoided." The chapter discussing ministry to the sick stresses the idea of the fellowship of the church which should "show special concern and responsibility." "The pastor and others . . . will pray with and for the patient." "They will help the patient . . . if need be, to approach death with calmness and hope." The Directory closes with a timely chapter on death and bereavement. "Christians recognize . . . the inevitability of death, but . . . they witness to their faith that God, in Jesus Christ, has conquered death." "The entire people of God" should uphold the bereaved. In funeral appointments, as in marriage ceremonies, "ostentation and undue expense are to be avoided." The funeral service "is a witness to God's promises in Jesus Christ, as attested by his resurrection from the dead, and to the sure and certain hope that he goes to prepare a place for his children."

In 1966, with the basic Directory thus completed and adopted by the church, the committee published *The Book of Common Worship—Provisional Services.* It was issued in temporary form in paperback with the request that comments and suggestions be made. Meanwhile, the General Assembly in 1961, on recommendation of the committee, had appointed a special committee to select hymns which would be bound together with the final worship book in a single volume. The Cumberland Presbyterian Church had entered into the cooperative undertaking, and in 1972 there was published with a changed name *The Worshipbook: Services and Hymns* under the joint auspices of the three cooperating Presbyterian bodies. *The Worshipbook* was also published without the hymns, for churches that preferred to use their own hymnals.

The book of course was for voluntary use. It sought to be both "Presbyterian" and "ecumenical." The General Assembly had asked the committee "to include . . . a significant percentage of hymns written in today's thought forms and styles, and hymns of black people." The committee appropriately offered the new book to the church "in the hope that it will serve a new age in the Church." The church responded heartily to the new book, and it soon enjoyed wide use.

By separate action the church amended the Constitution to permit baptized children who had not been received into full membership of the church to partake of the Lord's Supper if their local church session and their parents approved. By another action the church gave new emphasis to adult baptism on personal confession of faith and called attention of Presbyterians to the fact that this was a viable alternative to infant baptism.

Church Reorganization. The structure of the United Presbyterian Church underwent basic alterations in the same period that witnessed changes in the church's theological standards and in its worship guides. Similar structural reorganizations were undertaken by a number of other mainline denominations also in this same era.

The General Assembly of 1963, in response to an overture, created a Special Committee on Regional Synods and

Church Administration. During the next ten years the church was involved in reorganization, with attention focusing particularly on the two problems defined by this overture—synod realignment and restructuring of administration.

The committee directed its attention first to the problem of the urban church. Mainline Protestants were particularly conspicuous in the "flight to the suburbs," removing their resources from the inner city while continuing to benefit directly from the city as a center of business, transportation, communication, and culture. Demographers were describing metropolitan areas that included a core city and its satellite suburbs as a single economic and sociological unit. The Presbyterian Church had often talked about creating metropolitan presbyteries or synods, where the resources of the suburbs would be made more directly available for holding and outreach in the inner city. By 1963 all of the big-city presbyteries except New York included churches outside the city, but few, if any, included the total metropolitan area. With a very few exceptions, existing synod boundaries coincided with state lines, which sometimes distributed a single metropolitan area among two, and even three, states and synods.

The Assembly's committee seriously considered dividing the church into metropolitan synods but soon realized that vast areas of the United States did not lie within any metropolitan area. Meanwhile important changes were occurring in the nation and in the church. Long-standing racial injustice was attracting widespread attention and the Vietnam war was beginning to escalate alarmingly. Cynicism toward government, and toward central organizations in general, and an extreme localism were growing. Church membership and gifts to denominational enterprises in many mainline denominations including the Presbyterian were begin-

ning to decline. It was felt that if Presbyterian church government were made more representative of the grass roots,
and if as much as possible of the denominational program
were devolved to the various regions of the church, confidence would be restored. The thought of the committee
therefore turned from metropolitan synods to larger regional synods which could administer a large portion of the
denominational program and would be few enough so that
each synod could be represented on every major General
Assembly agency. Assuming that ministers and church
members would really identify with regional synods, the
plan would give greater consciousness of participation and
responsibility for work beyond the local parish and presbytery. The committee also had in view having every presbytery represented on every major agency of its regional
synod, thus making the regional synods central working
links between the General Assembly and the local presbyteries.

The Presbyterian Church was obviously in transition
during this national upheaval of the middle and late 1960's,
and the replies from more than a hundred synods and presbyteries, which the committee reported to the 1966 General
Assembly, showed that full consensus had not been
reached. Responses "ranged from complete endorsement
to complete rejection," but a majority did favor regional
synods, while not considering a restructuring of presbyteries to be necessary. The committee found the church to be
"clearly concerned to discover more effective ways of ac-
complishing its mission."

In a carefully prepared "Design for Mission" in 1968, the
committee not only reemphasized the desirability of regional synods but also spoke of the need for more efficient
"lines of administrative responsibility." The respective
judicatories should clearly determine policy for their ad-

ministrative agencies and should regularly review their work. A body representative of the General Assembly with the approval of the Assembly should set financial and other priorities for the whole church, and synods and presbyteries in descending order should set priorities for their constituents in the light of these denominational priorities. There would thus be a clear chain of command, and it was hoped that mere localism would be extended to larger objectives.

In 1969, the General Assembly, on recommendation of this committee, sent down to the presbyteries a series of amendments to the Form of Government, known as "Overture H," which the presbyteries adopted by a clear majority. This overture embodied many of the central principles of the previous year's "Design for Mission." The overture defined the mission roles of sessions and presbyteries in relation to the priorities of the denomination as a whole. It provided for the election by the synods of representatives to the General Assembly's agencies and gave additional powers of planning and oversight to the General Council of the General Assembly. It created an important council, the Council on Administrative Services, elected by the General Assembly "to establish policies for synod and presbytery administration"; "to counsel and concur" with synod and presbyteries, respectively, prior to the election of executives and staff members by those bodies; and to participate in the periodic review and evaluation of the chief executive officers of the General Assembly agencies and of synods and presbyteries. The provisions of the overture ensured the role of synod as the major link in expediting denominational priorities throughout the church.

The committee in this same year, 1969, recommended that the General Assembly create a Special Committee on Synod Boundaries and also a Special Committee on General Assembly Agencies; it then was discharged at its own request.

The new Special Committee on Synod Boundaries had been emphatically instructed "to undertake the widest possible consultation" with representatives of the existing synods and did so before redrawing synod lines in the interests of regionalization and decentralization. The committee soon came to the view that synods organized primarily according to metropolitan areas were not desired, but in no case did it allow an existing division of a metropolitan area among two or more synods to continue. It found a greater cherishing of the state boundaries of existing synods than had been anticipated, so that with very few exceptions the committee left the synods undivided, incorporating them in their wholeness into the new regional synods. By 1973 the entire church was realigned into fifteen regional synods, some of which were of vast territorial extent, often with comparatively few communicant members. Subsequently four synods, with membership of over 200,000, were each given an additional representative on the Program, Support, and Vocation Agencies.

The other committee for reorganization created by the General Assembly of 1969 was the Special Committee on General Assembly Agencies. The General Assembly agencies had not been drastically reorganized since 1923 when sixteen boards and agencies were consolidated into the Office of the General Assembly, the General Council, and four boards—National Missions, Christian Education, and Foreign Missions, the last-named merging in 1958 with the Permanent Commission on Interchurch Relation to form the Commission on Ecumenical Mission and Relations. As churches overseas had become or were becoming autonomous their problems increasingly resembled problems of the church at home. Services rendered by the boards of National Missions and Christian Education became more and more diversified with much overlapping. The result was a maze of interagency committees and communications. In addition, each of the boards was making its own promotional approach to congregations and judicatories at every level, resulting in much duplication of effort.

The Special Committee on General Assembly Agencies, construing its delegated powers broadly, had as its primary objective the greatest possible business efficiency in the conduct of the denominational enterprises. To this end, the committee defined two principal tasks—that of coordinating the total work of the church, and that of restructuring the General Assembly agencies.

For clearer coordination the committee greatly strengthened the General Council, changing its name to the General Assembly Mission Council, which of course remained directly subject to the General Assembly's review and control. This Council was given closer supervision and authority over all the Assembly's agencies. During these years of national upheaval and of tensions within the church itself this representative Council could be a powerful force for maintaining the church's unity by harmonizing varying viewpoints of the agencies which it supervised, perhaps on occasion at the price of retarding rapid change. Among its many other tasks the revised Council had the responsibility of proposing priorities and budgets for the entire church. As part of its ideal of united churchwide planning, the committee proposed a uniform system of accounting for the Assembly's agencies and for the judicatories that would be "compatible with the use of electronic data-processing equipment" and would make possible for the church "a common accounting language."

The committee also proposed restructuring the General

Assembly's agencies with the intent of avoiding overlapping and rivalry in promotion and of bringing together similar types of service in the same agencies. A new Program Agency combined the work of the former Board of National Missions, Board of Christian Education, and Commission on Ecumenical Mission and Relations, on the ground that "the fundamental nature of their relationships to the presbyteries and synods and overseas churches is very similar." Also it was felt that, by combining these three, greater flexibility could be achieved in redefining priorities and in shifting emphasis among the various types of service as changing needs might require. This of course involved a danger that promotion might thus be abstracted into the presentation of mere budgetary figures without presenting to potential donors the much greater appeal of specific human needs.

A Vocation Agency was created to serve the ever-changing roles of ministers and lay people and to combine the many diverse activities involved in preparing, guiding, and giving assistance to men and women engaged in professional services to the church. A Support Agency was created to provide integrated financial promotion, program interpretation, and stewardship development to the church at every level. These agencies should "work primarily with synods, and through synod with presbyteries." In general, "mission should be administered by the lowest judicatory that can effectively and efficiently handle it." But the Assembly itself should retain responsibility for such overall concerns as churchwide planning and budgeting, program guidance, national and international activities, and relations with the highest judicatories of other denominations.

In 1971 this Special Committee on General Assembly Agencies submitted to the Assembly amendments to the Constitution embodying its proposals which were decisively approved by the presbyteries. The committee also proposed that the Assembly create a Special Commission on the Reorganization of the General Assembly Agencies and was then discharged at its own request by the 1971 Assembly. The new Special Commission, having been empowered to make such adaptations as might be needed, implemented the new plans and completed its task in 1973. Thus after a full decade, and by the various activities of six different committees, the first major restructuring of the church's work in half a century was completed.

The Church and Education. In this same period the church developed a new Church Education Program. As compared with the *Christian Faith and Life* curriculum of 1948, it laid greater stress on preparatory instruction of teachers and parents both by the local church and by presbytery. It incorporated many of the more recent educational ideas which emphasized continuity of sequence in the material and concrete application to the student's total life situation. The context of worship was stressed, and help was provided for the student in reflecting on the meaning and application of what was taught.

The church maintained its traditionally strong interest in higher education. Amid extensive cultural change there was some debate as to what should be the distinctive contribution of a church-related college. The General Assembly of 1961 adopted a significant study on "The Church and Higher Education" which emphasized for its church-related colleges academic excellence, freedom of inquiry, and a critical spirit which would be both academic and prophetic. The report recalled the Reformed doctrine of Christian vocation and of concern that Christian values be creatively related to every area of human life and thought. The Assembly of 1976 reported that fifty-two colleges were officially related to the United Presbyterian Church.

European university students had long been politically active, but it was the Vietnam war that stimulated American youth to unprecedented involvement in public concerns. The General Assembly of 1970, in response to the new spirit, was the first Assembly to have "youth advisory delegates" from the presbyteries, with a voice but not a vote. The same Assembly urged that congregations elect an increased number of elders under the age of twenty-five and at every level give them a larger role in decision-making. Before long, most Assembly committees were giving the youth delegates a vote as well as a voice. In 1972 the Assembly voted to have also seminary advisory delegates—Presbyterian students elected by the student bodies of the church's seven seminaries—to have the same privileges as the youth advisory delegates. The innovation brought in fresh viewpoints and an additional link with a very important part of the church's constituency.

Theological seminaries through their student bodies felt the full impact of the Vietnam war. Over the longer term there was a tendency among many seminaries to return from a quite free elective system to more required work in basic areas, followed by electives. Ecumenical influences were strong, frequently resulting in joint programs with seminaries of other denominations which, particularly after the Second Vatican Council, often included Roman Catholic colleagues. Most seminaries changed their basic degree from Bachelor of Divinity to Master of Divinity, and many seminaries added a new earned Doctor of Ministry program for particularly well qualified pastors. The last-named degree was the capstone of expanding programs of continuing education which were everywhere in great demand in the face of continuing change in theological thinking and in ministerial functions.

Christian Unity. Ecumenicity entered a new era with the accession to the papacy of Pope John XXIII (1958) and his convening of the Second Vatican Council (1962–1965). In this period of change and flux, forces of modernity and the accumulated labors of theologians, Biblical scholars, liturgists, and others suddenly found new expression. Presbyterians and other Protestant and Orthodox churchmen were honored guests at the sessions of the Council. From its inception in 1948, the World Council of Churches had invited the Roman Catholic Church to join its work, and in 1961 the Vatican sent official observers to the World Council Assembly in New Delhi. Referring to the Second Vatican Council, the Presbyterian General Assembly of 1963 expressed gratitude to God "for these manifestations of Christian unity—an objective to which it has been committed by tradition since Calvin." The Assembly noted various "kinds of association with Roman Catholics which should be encouraged" such as "theological dialogues" and "social action at the civic level." In 1967 there began extended dialogues between Roman Catholics and members of the North American Area of the World Alliance of Reformed Churches to discuss theology, worship, and mission. Meanwhile Protestant and Roman Catholic seminaries were engaging in joint enterprises, and at the same time on the local community level many new forms of fellowship and cooperation were developing. Although of course basic differences remained, a quite new spirit of Christian goodwill was becoming widespread.

The World Alliance of Reformed Churches had been formed in 1875 with the participation of American Presbyterians who have been active in it ever since. In Nairobi, Kenya, in the summer of 1970 the Alliance united with the International Congregational Council to form the World Alliance of Reformed Churches (Presbyterian and Congregational). World Christianity today is predominantly composed not of isolated Christian congregations but of great worldwide denominational "families" having common heritages. The larger ecumenical movement itself involves study of the total Christian heritage from many perspectives in the search for mutual edification and agreement. The great denominational families, of which the Reformed is one of the largest and most important, have much of value to contribute to the common ecumenical enterprise.

What used to be called foreign missions was a chief precursor of the modern ecumenical movement, as the sending churches sought to find ways of cooperating rather than competing. Today the World Church aspires to a new ecumenical dimension, as the "older churches" and the "younger churches" enter into equal and mutually edifying dialogue and cooperation.

In 1961 the Presbyterian General Assembly invited the Protestant Episcopal Church to join with it in inviting the Methodist Church and the United Church of Christ to consider establishing "a united church truly Catholic, truly Reformed, and truly Evangelical." This resulted in a meeting of representatives of the four churches in 1962 which took the name "The Consultation on Church Union" (COCU). Two years later they declared: "We intend to stay together. . . . We have seen a vision of what Christian community in every place should be." By 1968 nine denominations were participating, and in 1970 a "Plan of Union" was distributed. The plan proposed a prominent role for bishops and the idealistic inclusion of socially and economically diverse local congregations under a single parish council. The latter provision seemed to offer the possibility of Christian fellowship across cultural lines, but many shrank from the apprehension that it would deprive the local congregation of control over its own policies and resources. At the same

time long-standing tradition still made Presbyterians shrink
from the very word "bishop," even though executive powers within the Presbyterian Church had been increasing for
a century and a half and the lack of constitutional power to
"place" pastors was leaving many ministers uprooted and
disillusioned. Widespread revolt against inclusive and powerful organizations of every kind was for the moment working against COCU and similar movements, but silent and
deeply rooted trends and needs still seemed to point ultimately toward greater unity and cooperation.

In the area of Christian unity the primary concern of
the United Presbyterian Church (Northern) was and had
been for many decades reunion with the Presbyterian
Church in the United States (Southern). The history of
negotiations between these two bodies has been discussed in detail in Chapter 11. Reunion negotiations
were resumed in 1969, but the years that immediately
followed were a time of national tension and of self-
study and reorganization in both churches. The two
General Assemblies in 1977, however, took a decided
forward step by agreeing to meet in the same city at the
same time in alternate years and to increase the area of
their cooperative work. Reunion itself was still in the future.

Finis. In this brief study we have seen the little church
planted by Jesus Christ become a world force. We have seen
it broken into numerous separate "churches," and have
traced the outline of one of the most important groups of
churches, the Presbyterian, with special reference to American Presbyterians. Presbyterians are only a part of the Kingdom, but they have their valuable contribution to make to
the common work for the Master. Pending the day of closer

cooperation, let each group serve the Christ faithfully with the special talents and heritage which it has received. So will the common task of all prosper most, and the Kingdom be most surely advanced.

Questions
for Thought
and Discussion

CHAPTER 1

In what sense might Presbyterianism be said to be as old as the apostles?

Could the early Christian martyrs have escaped death? How?

Were the conversion of the emperor and the official recognition of Christianity a gain or a loss for the Christian church? Give reasons.

What great military movement marks the beginning of the Middle Ages? What service did the Christian church perform amid the confusion of those invasions?

Name some of the noble achievements of the papacy in its early days; some of its bad effects in a later era.

What were the motives that caused people to go into monasteries?

Does the fact that Christ founded the church keep it free from error? Does the Christian church today need reform? Does it need revival?

CHAPTER 2

Was Martin Luther right or wrong when he taught that a person is accepted by God on the basis of faith alone? What did he mean by "faith"?

Does God today expect us to follow our individual consciences in preference to the commands of church and governmental authorities as Martin Luther did at the Diet of Worms? On the other hand, should we be willing to sacrifice for social convenience whims not based on intelligent conscience? What place does the Bible have in helping us to distinguish between true "conscience" and mere whim? What other helps are there for making this distinction?

Was Calvin correct in thinking of Christianity as a direct relationship to Christ as a living person?

What do you think of Calvin's idea of the church as a disciplined community? Is the church of today too indifferent toward inconsistencies of life and toward antisocial practices of Christians?

What duties does a Christian today have to his community and to his nation? Was Calvin right that these duties are limited by a higher duty to God?

Can an earnest Christian worship God better through an elaborate ritual or through a simpler ritual?

CHAPTER 3

Did the organization of their church strengthen the Huguenots? Is the church as an organization necessary today? Are there dangers from excessive organization?

In persecuting the Huguenots what did the French government lose economically? morally? religiously? Did any permanent gain result from this policy of persecution?

Can you see any connection between the bloodthirsty persecutions of Huguenots and the atheism of the French Revolution which followed? Does our conduct as individual Christians and as a church today have any effect in drawing people to Christ or in repelling them from him?

Why, do you suppose, did businessmen incline to favor religious toleration? Did Holland gain by granting religious toleration? Did Holland's religious toleration help other countries? Was anything lost?

In the lands of Europe where Presbyterianism never did secure a permanent foothold, do you think the labors and sufferings of the early Presbyterian workers were wasted? Explain.

CHAPTER 4

After reading about Knox's "call," how do you think God "calls" people today to the Christian ministry? Does God "call" people to nonprofessional Christian service? How does he "call"?

Is any government justified in trying to change a people's religion by force, as James I and Charles I sought to do in Scotland? What should a Christian do if a government tries to dictate his religious faith by force?

Do you think that any of the Christian denominations of America should be merged, following the example of the Scottish churches? Name some.

Why are the people of northern Ireland sometimes called "Scotch-Irish"? Do you think that the Catholics of Ulster were fairly treated?

Are there causes of tension between Protestants and Roman Catholics in America today? What can be done to promote goodwill?

CHAPTER 5

Is it possible today to bring all Christians to believe alike and to worship alike, as Queen Elizabeth tried to do? Is it desirable? Is it possible for Christians to practice mutual goodwill and cooperation while still retaining their various differences of belief and worship? Name some problems involved in attempting to do this.

Has Christianity contributed to the rise of political democracy? Can you see any parallels between political democracy and Christian principles? What differences do you find?

From what country was English Presbyterianism replenished? Tell the story.

After reading about the founding of Presbyterianism in Wales, do you think that religious revivals can have permanent results?

Do you think the British Commonwealth nations are likely to assume an increasingly important place in world history? If so, what is the potential importance of the flourishing Presbyterianism among them?

As you look at the statistics of Worldwide Presbyterianism what do they suggest to you about this family of churches and its relative strength in different areas of the world?

CHAPTER 6

What combination of events made it certain that England's American colonies would be predominantly Protestant?

What racial groups brought Presbyterianism to America?

Give reasons from early American church history why Presbyterianism today is numerically weak in New England and numerically strong in the Middle Atlantic States.

Does the Presbyterian Church today reflect the inclusive spirit implied in the diversity of the first presbytery?

How did the "from the ground up" organization of the first presbytery point toward democratic church government?

What caused Presbyterians in colonial America to favor religious toleration? Did they gain or lose by toleration? Are there moral implications in the issue of religious toleration?

CHAPTER 7

Name some reasons for the growth of early American Presbyterianism.

Would more of the early Presbyterian seriousness and reverence benefit our church life today?

Does the spirit of the Adopting Act of 1729 still have something to teach us today?

Will a true Christian necessarily be able to point to the date of his or her conversion, as some of the leaders of the Great Awakening taught? If not, what is the distinguishing characteristic of a Christian?

Is emotion harmful or beneficial to the Christian life? Illustrate your answer from the Great Awakening.

Which is easier in church work, division or cooperation? Which serves the Kingdom better?

Should the frontier missionaries be numbered among the heroes of Christian history? Give reasons.

CHAPTER 8

What was the attitude of Presbyterians toward the cause of American independence?

Tell something of the contribution of the Presbyterian Church to religious toleration in America.

By 1788 the Presbyterian Church possessed five documents as standards. Name the five. Name the four church courts, or judicatories, of which the General Assembly is the highest.

Give your impressions of the revival of 1798–1801. What were some of its good effects?

What were the chief causes of the church's remarkable growth during the period covered by this chapter?

CHAPTER 9

Name some of the possible ways that Christians might have organized the new missionary, reforming, and other activities of the early nineteenth century. What were the advantages and disadvantages of conducting these by nondenominational voluntary societies? What were the advantages and disadvantages of having the church itself conduct these activities? In what ways have these continuing activities affected the organization and life of the church in the late twentieth century?

What were the advantages of the Plan of Union of 1801? State the relation of a local church under the Plan to the Congregational and Presbyterian denominations respectively.

State some of the results accomplished by Mills and his haystack meeting. Name some practical ways in which young people today can devote their lives to Christian service.

Describe the conditions that confronted frontier missionaries. What does America of today owe them?

Can education, by itself, make a person a Christian? How can education make a person a more useful Christian?

CHAPTER 10

Name some of the changes that appeared in American public life around 1830; some parallel changes in church life.

Do you find any parallels between the church's attitude toward slavery in the early nineteenth century and the church's attitude toward quite different social issues in the late twentieth century? What problems are involved in the church's treatment of social issues?

Do you think the Presbyterian Church gained anything by dividing in 1837? What did it lose? Do the issues that divided the church in 1837 seem important today?

What lands were added to the United States during this period? Did the churches meet the new responsibility? Explain.

Tell the story of the separation of the Southern Church. What ties continue to bind these sister denominations?

CHAPTER 11

Describe the circumstances under which the independent "Presbyterian Church in the Confederate States of America" was organized.

Name some of the distinctive characteristics of this Southern Presbyterian Church.

Trace over the years the developing relations between the Southern and Northern Presbyterian Churches. What factors have hindered these relations? What factors have fostered these relations?

What internal changes—other than in its relations with the

Northern Church—do you see in the Southern Presbyterian Church over the years?

In what ways do you find both the Southern and the Northern Presbyterian Churches influenced by the sections in which their chief strength lies? In what ways are these two churches influencing their respective areas?

CHAPTER 12

Name some factors that helped to reunite Old School and New School Presbyterians. Are any of these forces operating to unite denominations today?

When a Christian's beliefs are challenged by new ideas, what should he or she do about it? In what ways might such a crisis strengthen Christian faith? How might it deepen spiritual life?

What was the effect on the church's life and beliefs of retaining the Westminster Confession with minimal amendments instead of writing a contemporary statement of the church's faith?

How can the church help business and labor to understand each other better? to work for the welfare of all?

What special problems has the growth of cities created for the church? What special opportunities?

List some things that your local church could do to improve the relations among the churches in your community.

What is to be said in favor of formal, read worship? in favor of a simpler, more spontaneous service? What is essential for any true Christian worship?

CHAPTER 13

What do you think should be the Christian's attitude toward war? Can a universal answer be given, or must the answer vary with each war? Can civil government be expected to leave to individuals the decision as to what wars they can and what wars they cannot support?

What is the difference between belief about God and trust in God? Are both necessary for the Christian? Explain.

Name local forces that are making relations better between different denominations in your own community. Name forces that increase separation among them.

To Christianize peoples in other lands, is it necessary to Americanize them? How can we help them to develop a Christianity of their own? What can we learn from these younger churches and how can we learn it?

How should the church try to influence American industrial life?

Does the church have economic involvements of its own, and is it adequately Christianizing these?

Are there ways in which Christian faith should limit patriotism? ways in which it should increase patriotism?

In your community is the church leading or lagging in racial desegregation? How do you explain this?

Name some of the advances in women's rights in the Presbyterian Church in recent decades. What still remains to be done?

Can you see any connection between the emphasis of the Presbyterian and Reformed Churches on the Bible and their strong emphasis on education?

CHAPTER 14

In what ways did the Covenanters and Seceders show courage and Christian devotion in Scotland and in America? (See also Chapter 4.)

Did their strong convictions create any difficulties? What should be the attitude today of a Christian toward social customs that some people consider morally or spiritually dubious? By what tests should the Christian decide this question?

What were some of the problems faced by pioneer home missionaries and foreign missionaries? What were their rewards?

What does the history of the United Presbyterian Church of

North America teach about how to achieve Christian unity? What spirit is necessary? What should be sacrificed for larger Christian unity? What may not properly be sacrificed?

Of what importance was the merger of 1958 that created The United Presbyterian Church in the U.S.A.? What can you do that this church may have greater influence for Jesus Christ?

CHAPTER 15

List some things that you and your congregation might do in the interests of greater racial justice in your community. Is your language and conversation on the side of racial equality?

In times of crisis are you merely critical, or do you have constructive alternatives to propose? From a Christian perspective, what do you think should be America's role in the world today?

What is the percentage of women on your local church session? How many of these chair committees? How many women pastors are there in your presbytery?

It would be interesting to compare the five Reformation era documents (Scots, Heidelberg, Second Helvetic, and two Westminster) of the Presbyterian Church's *Book of Confessions* as to the sequence and content of their respective treatments of such topics as Scripture, God the Father, Son, Holy Spirit, church, redemption, and Christian duty. What do you consider to be the strongest features in the Confession of 1967?

Name some kinds of activity that the idea of a Christian ministry by all lay people suggests to you.

Would you like to see the Lord's Supper more frequently celebrated? Why, or why not? What kinds of public worship services do you find most helpful?

What needs did the reorganization of Presbyterian synods and agencies between 1963 and 1973 seek to meet?

How would you define the ideal objectives of a church-related college? What kind of influence do young adults have in your local congregation and presbytery?

Define the purposes of the ecumenical movement. Under what circumstances are denominational mergers desirable? Have relations between Protestants and Roman Catholics become more understanding and constructive in your community in recent years? Explain.

Bibliography

In the foregoing study, statistics for churches outside the United States are from the World Alliance of Reformed Churches (Presbyterian and Congregational), *Membership Statistics: August, 1974.* Mimeographed. Office of the Alliance, Geneva, Switzerland.

Background Studies

Ahlstrom, Sydney E., *A Religious History of the American People.* Yale University Press, 1972.

Handy, Robert T., *A History of the Churches in the United States and Canada.* Oxford University Press, 1977.

Hudson, Winthrop S., *Religion in America.* 2d ed. Charles Scribner's Sons, 1973.

Kerr, Hugh T., Jr., *Positive Protestantism: A Return to First Principles.* Prentice-Hall, 1963.

Marty, Martin E., *A Short History of Christianity.* Collins-World, 1959.

McNeill, John T., *The History and Character of Calvinism.* Oxford University Press, 1954.

Morison, Samuel Eliot, *The Oxford History of the American People.* Oxford University Press, 1965.

Nichols, James Hastings, *Primer for Protestants.* Greenwood, 1947.

Parker, T. H., *John Calvin: A Biography.* The Westminster Press, 1976.

Walker, Williston, *A History of the Christian Church*. 3d edition, edited by Robert T. Handy. Charles Scribner's Sons, 1970.

American Presbyterianism

Armstrong, M. W., Loetscher, L. A., and Anderson, C. A. (eds.), *The Presbyterian Enterprise: Sources of American Presbyterian History*. The Presbyterian Historical Society, 1956.

Briggs, Charles A., *American Presbyterianism: Its Origin and Early History*. Charles Scribner's Sons, 1885.

Dowey, Edward A., Jr., *A Commentary on the Confession of 1967 and an Introduction to The Book of Confessions*. The Westminster Press, 1968.

Hoge, Dean R., *Division in the Protestant House*. The Westminster Press, 1976.

Jamison, Wallace N., *The United Presbyterian Story: A Centennial Study*. The Geneva Press, 1958.

Lake, Benjamin J., *The Story of the Presbyterian Church in the U.S.A.* The Westminster Press, 1956.

Loetscher, Lefferts A., *The Broadening Church: A Study of Theological Issues in the Presbyterian Church Since 1869*. University of Pennsylvania Press, 1954.

Miller, Park Hays, *Why I Am a Presbyterian*. Thomas Nelson & Sons, 1956.

Murray, Andrew E., *Presbyterians and the Negro—A History*. The Presbyterian Historical Society, 1966.

Nichols, Robert Hastings, *Presbyterianism in New York State: A History of the Synod and Its Predecessors*. Edited and completed by James Hastings Nichols. The Westminster Press, 1963.

Sweet, William Warren, *Religion on the American Frontier*, Vol. II of *The Presbyterians, 1783–1840*. Harper & Brothers, 1936.

Thompson, Ernest Trice, *Presbyterians in the South*. 3 vols. John Knox Press, 1963–1973.

Thompson, Robert E., *A History of the Presbyterian Churches in the United States*. Charles Scribner's Sons, 1895.

Trinterud, Leonard J., *The Forming of an American Tradition: A Re-*

examination of Colonial Presbyterianism. The Westminster Press, 1949.

Attention should be called to the Presbyterian Historical Society, 5th and Lombard Streets, Philadelphia, Pennsylvania, which has extensive Presbyterian historical collections, open to the public. The Society publishes a quarterly, *Journal of Presbyterian History,* devoted to aspects of Presbyterian history. The Society also publishes from time to time monographs on Presbyterian history in its Presbyterian Historical Society Publication Series.

Topical Index

This book is a historical study and it is therefore structured in chronological order. But its contents may also be studied topically by the aid of the following index.

Theology, worship, church organization, and social concern (including sociological character) go far toward describing the distinctive features of any religion or denomination. These four categories, therefore, constitute the key entries of the topical index given below. A study of these four aspects will reveal much of the distinctive character of American Presbyterianism. In what ways do you find each of these four characteristics influencing each of the others? In what ways, for example, has Presbyterian theology influenced Presbyterian worship, organization, and social concern? Similarly, in what ways have worship, organization, and social concern, respectively, influenced each of the others?

It would be interesting also to compare resemblances and differences between Presbyterianism and other leading denominations in respect to each of these four characteristics, and to notice how greatly resemblances predominate over differences, especially in recent decades. (Standard encyclopedias provide individual articles on leading denominations. Indexes in histories of American Christianity, some of which works are listed in the bibliography of this book, point to much information on individual denominations, as do especially numerous denominational monographs.)

History involves process and change and also interrelation between the subject studied and its larger environment. Church history is the study of God's working through fallible human beings in this process and amid these interrelations. Each of the four central characteristics mentioned above has, to a degree, a history of its own. In what ways, for example, do you find the church's theological views changing over the centuries? How did these changes affect the church's environment and how were they affected by the environment? Similar questions concerning the church's worship, organization, and social concern, respectively, could lead to interesting insights and fresh conclusions. Use of a good social or general history of the United States—such as that, for example, listed in the accompanying bibliography—would be helpful for additional information concerning the larger American environment as the context in which the church's changes and interactions have occurred.

Boards, church. *See* Church government and organization

Church and state: under Constantine, 12; in Middle Ages, 16; Calvin on, 26; in France, 30–31; in the Netherlands, 33; in Scotland, 38–42; in Ireland, 43; toleration in England, 51; in middle colonies, 59; favored by American Presbyterians, 62, 75–76; Southern Presbyterians, 106, 114–115. *See also* Civil government

Church, doctrine of. *See* Theology

Church government and organization: papal, 16, 19–20, 21–22; Calvin's presbyterianism, 25–26; four judicatories, 29; in Scotland, 39; in Ireland, 43–44; Puritans on, 48–50; in Wales, 54; in early New England, 58–59; an American presbytery, 61; a synod, 63; a General Assembly, 76–77; parallels to civil government, 77–78; voluntary societies and church boards, 82–84, 96, 98–100; in the South, 106–107, 116; in the UPNA, 153; Plan of Union, 85–86, 96, 97; elders, 107; centralization, 108; financial promotion, 108, 116, 138; reorganization in 1973, 173–180; youth delegates, 181. *See also* Church and state; Education; Ministry; Missions; Unity and disunity; Women's work

Civil government: Calvin on, 26; Puritans on, 50–51; social contract, 50, 73–74. *See also* Church and State

Clergy. *See* Ministry

Colleges. *See* Education

Communism. *See* Social concern

Cooperation of Christians. *See* Unity and disunity

Decline, religious: after church establishment, 12; in late Middle Ages, 19–20, 21–22; following the American Revolution, 79; after the 1950's, 157. *See also* Revival, religious

Democracy. *See* Civil government

Divisions, church. *See* Unity and disunity

Doctrine. *See* Theology

Ecumenical movement. *See* Unity and disunity

Education: monasteries, 14; Calvin on, 27; English dissenters, 52; colonial, 65–67; theological seminaries, 90–91, 120, 147, 152, 181; colleges, 101–102, 119–120, 146, 152, 180; Sunday church schools and curriculum, 90, 119, 145–146, 180

Foreign missions. *See* Missions

Home missions. *See* Missions

Laity. *See* Ministry

Ministry: secularized, 12; a distinct class, 16; marriage of, 23; Calvin on, 25; Knox "called" to, 37; executive functions and parity of clergy, 83; lay influence in voluntary societies, 84; ministry and laity restudied, 166–169. *See also* Monasteries

Missions: in early church, 11; in Middle Ages, 15; to American Indians, 69; to frontiers, 71, 81, 149; structure of, 82–84; church as a missionary society, 99; foreign missions, 86–87, 117–118, 141–143, 153; home missions, 87–90. *See also* Church government and organization

Monasteries: cultural influence, 14; virtues and faults, 17, 18; Luther a monk, 21; Luther's marriage, 23

North-South Presbyterian relations. *See* Unity and disunity

Organization. *See* Church government and organization

Peace movements. *See* Social concern

Persecution: of early Christians, 11; of "heretics," 12; of Protestants, 24, 30, 32

Polity. *See* Church government and organization

Race, church and. *See* Social concern

Religious liberty. *See* Church and state

Revival, religious: in Wales, 53; Great Awakening, 67–69, 71; Second Great Awakening, 78–80; as a unitive force, 90; nineteenth century, 119, 151; after World War II, 139, 157. *See also* Decline, religious

Rural problems. *See* Social concern

Slavery. *See* Social concern

Social concern: in ancient church, 12; Calvin on, 27; in England after 1688, 51; structuring of, 82–84; slavery issue, 92–95, 97, 99, 151–152; "spirituality" of the church, 109, 122; industrial and urban issues, 121, 132–134, 143; racial issues, 121–122, 144, 152, 157–159; rural problems, 134, 144; Communism, 139; peace movements, 138,

159–160; Life and Work, 141; miscellaneous. *See also* Education; Wars

"Spirituality" of the church. *See* Social concern

Subscription to creed. *See* Theology

Sunday schools. *See* Education

Theological seminaries. *See* Education

Theology: in ancient church, 13–14; salvation by faith, 21, 23; Calvin, 24; Arminianism, 34; Arianism and Unitarianism, 45, 52; Anglican theology, 47; Westminster Confession, 49–50; subscription to Westminster Confession, 45, 64–65, 77, 165; doctrine of the church, 83; Enlightenment impact, 92; New School theology, 96, 110; Biblical criticism and evolution, 120–121, 129–130; creedal change, 120–121; fundamentalism, 132; neo-orthodoxy, 140; Faith and Order, 141; UPNA, 151, 153–154; Confession of 1967, 162–166. *See also* Revival, religious

Toleration, religious. *See* Church and state

Unity and disunity: Calvin on Christian unity, 24; Scottish unions, 42; Presbyterian-

Congregational cooperation, 52; English unions, 53; Canadian unions, 54–55; reunion of 1758, 70; Cumberland reunion, 80; early nineteenth century, 82–84, 95; Old School–New School division, 92, 95–97; New School church divides, 99; Old School church divides, 102–106; North-South Presbyterian relations, 102–106, 112–114, 118, 122–126, 127–128, 184; reunion in the South, 110; reunion in the North, 128–129; federations, 125, 135, 142, 182; church mergers, 135–136; UPNA, 150–151, 154–155; UPUSA, 155–156; ecumenical relations, 125, 140–142, 182–184

Voluntary societies. *See* Church government and organization

Wars: Crusades, 18–19; French Revolution, 31; English Civil War, 49; Glorious Revolution, 51; American Revolution, 73–75, 149; American Civil War, 104–105, 109, 110–112, 115, 127–128, 152; World War I, 116, 137–138; World War II, 139, 143–144; Vietnam war, 159–160

Women's work, 116–117, 144–145, 146, 152, 161

Worldwide Presbyterianism, statistics, 56

Worship: before the Reformation, 12, 17–18; Calvin on, 27; Puritan ideals of, 48; colonial, 65–66; in the nineteenth century, 119; in the twentieth century, 119, 136, 169–173